MW00984851

The 2020-2021 Edition

College Essay
Master Guide

For Ivy League and Elite Applications

PREPVANTAGE

- Please visit PrepVantageTutoring.com for additional study materials and information regarding future book releases

ISBN-13: 979-8638475031

Visit us at **PrepVantageTutoring.com**

The College Essay Master Guide: 2020-2021 Edition
Copyright © 2020 PrepVantage Publishing

ISBN-13: 979-8638475031

Table of Contents

Introduction

"Eventually, the essay is everything."

Dear student,

This book is premised on one of the most important rules not only of the college application essay, but also of another important step towards the best possible college acceptances. If you have studied for the PSAT, SAT, or ACT, you have probably spent plenty of time figuring out exactly *why* you answered specific questions incorrectly. After all, if you can't figure out where you are going wrong, you can't figure out how to go right.

Right and wrong, strengths and weaknesses—this is the best mentality for considering the college application essay itself. After all, if anything is fundamentally wrong with an essay, that essay and the application it came with can all too easily get thrown straight into the reject pile. There are, in today's competitive college environment, 20,000 more where that came from.

Yes, this is the logical way of thinking about college essays. Unfortunately, it is not a way of thinking that is as popular as it should be.

Too often, students are offered too little in the way of direction or critique: guidance counselors and even paid college consultants can vaguely exhort applicants to "express themselves" or to "write about what they care about." Yet today's high school students aren't merely looking for self-expression—far from it. They are looking for essays that will garner acceptances to schools that accept under 7%

of all applicants. Self-expression can be part of it, but is not really the goal itself; even brainstorming can and must be disciplined and systematic.

Again unfortunately, the experience of editing the college essay is sometimes little better. Too much of the advice that is currently on the market revolves around grammar, proofreading, transitions: all important matters, but NOT the ones that can lift an essay to excellence. The best essays are masterpieces of description, emotion, and narrative structure—matters that no amount of spellchecking can conjure into existence.

So, here's the question: how can you escape writing an essay that seems decent but is in fact self-destructively mediocre, and *instead* write an essay that will get you accepted to the school of your dreams?

There is a way to improve your odds: a coherent, streamlined strategy for getting inside the heads of admissions officers—who after all want to be entertained and impressed, just like any other subset of readers. Writing a standout essay won't be easy. It will require deeper thought and reflection than you may be used to with a standard five-paragraph argumentative paper. But it will be straightforward, a matter of what can go wrong and of how to set your ideas right, from your first brainstorm to your first sentence to, eventually, your first acceptance letter.

Welcome to the Master Guide to the College Essay.

-PrepVantage

Part 1

Planning Your Personal Statement

Essay Fundamentals

What to Do, and What NEVER to Do

This book was created for students who, despite their obvious talents, are nonetheless in a tricky position. Often, the challenge that they face isn't a matter of GPA, test scores, or extracurriculars. All of those of those can be solid, or phenomenal. The real question that even a student with a 4.0 and 10 AP courses, a 1590 on the SAT and a national merit scholarship, and a bunch of varsity letters and a profitable tech startup on his or her resume must ask requires intense self-awareness:

- *How do I write an essay that will effectively capture my life and character?*

In terms of the fundamentals, many students know that they need to create an essay that conveys something interesting or admirable from the standpoint of personality, and that doesn't simply regurgitate resume items. Those are the ground rules that every worthwhile book, every worthwhile college essay coach will give you.

Nonetheless, those concise rules STILL leave plenty of room for a college essay, from even the best student, to go completely wrong. That is what happens to too many college applicants today, brilliant and talented high school students who are given advice that does nothing but lead their essays completely off track. This book is designed to keep you on the right path.

The Personal Statement: Ground Rules

The core requirement of almost any college application that you file, regardless of school or program, will be a personal statement; this essay normally runs between 450 and 650 words. Within those 650 or so words, you will need to

1. **Present a side of your personality that the college of your choice will admire and see as an asset**

2. **Deliver a narrative that is well-structured, vivid, and enjoyable on its own terms**

There are many ways to meet these two objectives: in fact, the combinations of personality, topic, and description that you can come up with are manifold. You have plenty of liberty, but you must realize that (barring a miracle, or an incredibly lenient essay reader) some topics will NEVER be effective.

AVOID: The Worst Topics

Although self-expression is an important part of any college essay, there are a few major though often unspoken restrictions. The first is that, self-expression or no self-expression, there are topics that you should almost NEVER write about. These topics may be important to you in real life; they may in fact be essential parts of your life story. Still, you must avoid them, completely.

Here are a few of the absolute worst college essay topics.

- Grades ⊠

Your academic performance will get enough emphasis thanks to your transcripts and recommendations. But even if this weren't the case, grades are an incredibly dull topic. You didn't enjoy cramming for Honors Trigonometry; why would your reader enjoy reading about it?

- Test Scores ⊠

Possibly the most unoriginal topic on the planet. Almost EVERY high-achieving college applicant had to study for the SAT or ACT in some form. That studying probably wasn't fun to begin with, and even if you did by some miracle enjoy it, writing about a topic as commonplace as test scores is a complete failure of initiative and imagination.

- The College Essay Itself ⊠

It's really sad if so little happened in the life of a high school student, any high school student, that "writing the personal statement" is a major event. It's not: it's a college requirement, and an important one, but NOT the kind of thing that makes for an interesting essay. Don't try writing a quirky meta-essay for this one either. No amount of verbal cleverness will veil the fact that this is a woefully dry and painfully obvious topic.

- Dead Relatives $\boxed{X}$

Almost everyone has lost a relative at some point: it is a saddening experience, but NOT one that will make your application stand out. There are other dangers here, from the fact that this topic can quickly become over-emotional and poorly organized, to the fact that it can completely cloud YOUR OWN personality in favor of the relative's. Just avoid it.

- Dead Pets $\boxed{X}$

All the problems with dead relatives, but maybe even worse. You are more likely to wind up with an essay that is both overly sentimental and completely un-extraordinary than with the next *Marley and Me*—and, alas, there were plenty of people who didn't like *Marley and Me* anyway. Let deceased dogs lie.

You have probably noticed that these topics have two things in common.

1. **They may reveal a positive side of you.**

2. **They will certainly bore a reader to death.**

You need to keep in mind, always, that your essay is being viewed by admissions readers who don't simply want smart or competent students. These readers want students who are exciting, original, intriguing, creative: these are the personality traits, after all, that allow high intelligence to achieve its full potential.

Other essay topics will self-destruct for the opposite reasons: they are too controversial, provocative, or dark for their own good. You will also need to avoid the following under almost ALL circumstances.

- Suicide ☒

- Drug/Alcohol/Substance Use ☒

- Abuse of Any Sort ☒

- Sexual Activity of Any Sort ☒

- Severe Mental Illness of Any Sort ☒

At first, the fact that these topics should be more or less banned may seem unfair, arbitrary, and insensitive. There are so many works of great literature that revolve around one, a few, or all of these: writings ranging from *Hamlet* to *Crime and Punishment* to *The Catcher in the Rye* would not even exist without such topics. And these topics may be real struggles for you, the major hurdles that have defined your life in high school.

The trick as always is that the essay should

1. **advertise your BEST possible qualities while**

2. **doing NOTHING that would make a reader seriously question your judgment or maturity.**

Even an insightful, honest, well-written discussion of a struggle with mental illness or substance abuse will be likely to defeat both of these purposes, automatically.

But can you talk about somebody else's dark life?

Yes, yes you can. In fact, some students write very good essays about rising above families and communities with major problems. For instance, if you helped a close friend through thoughts of suicide, helped set up a peer counseling hotline, and want to become a psychiatrist, you would be insane not to talk about such valuable work in some form.

HOWEVER, there are bunch of things you should make sure NOT to do, including

- Sounding preachy or condescending

- Trying to make yourself look perfect

- Going to great lengths to shock the reader

- Losing sight of your own character

Avoid all of these liabilities and you will be in excellent shape; you will have an essay that approaches thought-provoking problems but does not wallow in them. And for how EXACTLY you might write an application essay while taking only the most necessary risks, consult the "Breaking the Rules" strategies that appear in Chapter 4.

Working with the Prompt

So if you need to avoid this many topics—including some that may be extremely important to you in your life beyond the essay—what CAN you write about? Here are a few of the topics that have been featured in recent Common Application prompts.

- **A place where you feel at peace or can be yourself**

- **A challenge or a difficulty that you have overcome**

- **An idea that you have questioned or opposed**

- **A problem that you would like to solve or address**

- **A topic of your choice**

As you can see, these topics do offer direction: an essay about a "challenge" or "problem" will naturally have a classic plot arc of some sort. But how you zero in on the exact challenge or problem that you would like to discuss is not especially easy. In fact, some applications will finish with a section asking if there is "anything additional" that you would like to write about—a question that is so broad and open-ended that answering it can do much more harm than good.

Instead of trying to answer the specific application questions right off the bat, do this: forget that the questions even exist and figure out what you would IDEALLY like to write about. Personal statement and especially Common Application prompts are often broad enough that any acceptable topic you pick will probably fit at least one of them—and often more than one.

To start figuring out your best possible topic or topics, just use the topic questionnaire that begins on the next page. It will help you to put your interests, passions, and background in perspective, and in manageable form. And it just might save you hours of staring at a blank Microsoft Word document and wondering what to write.

The Profile-at-a-Glance
QUESTIONNAIRE

DIRECTIONS: Respond to the questions quickly and honestly, without worrying about judgment of any sort at this point. Truthful answers will help you to determine what material you can REALLY discuss in an inspired or passionate manner.

Part 1: Your Activities

If you could only continue ONE of your current activities in college, you would choose: _____

Why?: _____

If you could take up a hobby or activity that you are NOT currently pursuing, you would choose: _____

Why?: _____

Which of your activities has been MOST fulfilling?: _____
_____

Why?: _____

Which of your activities has been LEAST fulfilling?: _____
_____

Why?: _____

In one sentence, what is the most valuable lesson that you have learned from one of your activities?: _____

_____

_____

Part 2: Your Personality

If you had to pick ONLY THREE of your personal strengths, what would they be? Select and circle three (or fewer) terms from the list below and trust your first instincts; DO NOT over-think this writing task.

Resilient	Patient	Outspoken
Creative	Entrepreneurial	Empathetic
Sociable	Self-Aware	Spontaneous
Versatile	Loyal	Pragmatic
Self-Sacrificing	Able to Accept Criticism	
Calm under Pressure	Capable of Transformation	
Eager to Take Risks	Fascinated by New Ideas	

Want another shot at the Questionnaire?

If you do, all you have to do is turn to the back of this book (Pages 118-121). You will find two additional copies of the Profile Questionnaire. Give yourself a re-do, or two.

Now that you have completed the Essay Questionnaire, you should have a manageable overview of both your profile and your personality. But don't get ready to write your personal statement just yet. There are still a few high-danger topics left: fortunately, you will be able to see them much better (and understand why they go wrong) with the questionnaire as your guide.

WARNING: Cliché Topics

The truth about student profiles is that not all activities are created equal. Some experiences, in fact, have been so badly over-used on college essays that they are now regarded as clichés—and should, unless you are desperate for a topic or willing to take a risk, be avoided.

It is true that you may have deep experience with some of these cliché topics; some of the issues and emotions that they raise may even be enormously meaningful to you. Yet some of these subjects, for the reasons outlined in the segment that follows, are no longer meaningful to the admissions officials reading your applications.

- Minor Trips Abroad ☒

Don't take it from this book alone: take it from *New York Times* columnist Frank Bruni, who found that college students are over-using narratives about doing good in "exotic locations" to impress admissions officers. Bruni's entire discussion (published as "To Get to Harvard, Go to Haiti?") can be found at https://www.nytimes.com/2016/08/14/opinion/sunday/to-get-to-harvard-go-to-haiti.html. For now, it is enough to say that "I spent a week in [insert faraway, problem-afflicted country here] and it changed my life!" is a premise that can seem superficial and insulting to many admissions committees. Why not discover your OWN community and solve some of its problems?

- Physical Ailments $\boxed{X}$

One of the personal least favorite topics for some readers: for every 20 essay drafts about physical ailments, maybe one will be worth not throwing out immediately. The topic is badly over-used, and in most cases, by dwelling on an affliction or injury, a writer will suggest the OPPOSITE of determination and initiative. Essays about physical ailments can also become sentimental and self-pitying. Unless you can stay upbeat, hopeful, and strong willed when composing one of these—the very, VERY rare exception—just avoid.

- Being Undecided About Your Future $\boxed{X}$

You may honestly not know what you want to do with the rest of your life, or even with your choice of major. Fair enough. However, dedicating an entire essay to such uncertainties will most likely result in vague and poorly-organized writing—and will undermine your ability to communicate qualities such as passion and determination.

- Anything (Unvetted) in a Strange Format $\boxed{X}$

Want to write the essay as a poem, as a set of journal entries, or as a television script? You can try; you will run a high risk of failure. Essays in such strange formats sometimes grab a reader's attention, though the risk of getting an inhospitable reader often outweighs the chance of getting a more accepting one. The BIGGER risk is trying to have an interesting format hold up an essay that, otherwise, is uninteresting. You must formulate the best ideas possible, and you cannot neglect that task to write an otherwise bland essay formatted as a collection of sonnets or a letter to an imaginary friend.

Of course, there's that "Unvetted" part. As you will learn in Chapter 4, strange formats can indeed work. Some of these formats have succeeded brilliantly in real life, but you NEED outside readers to let you know if yours is doing so too.

But can a Cliché Topic ever work?

There are a few circumstances under which you might not get completely demolished for picking a cliché topic. These are:

1) If the rest of your application is good enough to make a well-worded but otherwise mediocre essay excusable (unlikely at the most competitive schools)

2) If the style and descriptions are so powerful that the weak topic and theme are overlooked (uncommon, but possible even with the deadly "Being Undecided" cliché, as explained on Pages 71-72)

3) If you blow up the cliché (which is tricky but can DEFINITELY be pulled off well)

As you can probably guess, Circumstance 3 is the unusual one. In fact, it is one of the possibilities that you can explore in the "Opening Sentences" segment on Pages 41-43. But don't flip forward just yet: you need to figure out how more reliable essays are constructed before you can start taking dynamite to College Essay clichés.

CHOOSE: Acceptable Topics

You have now avoided all of the main personal statement pitfalls. Now, take a second look at your Profile Questionnaire, then consider the top two or three interests and activities that you might want to write about.

To make all this more manageable, use the list form below.

Interests and Activities

1) _____

2) _____

3) _____

Do the same right now with your personality traits: choose the strongest or (perhaps better) most interesting ones.

Character Traits

1) _____

2) _____

3) _____

If you want, you can begin piecing together how you might talk about a few of these topics. However, you should be aware that even acceptable topics can backfire. Even these have their strengths and weaknesses.

To see why this is so—and what EXACTLY those strengths and weaknesses are—consider the Pros and Cons of some of the most common Interests and Activities. All of these have been used in successful essays. All of them can also run into problems unless you think them through sufficiently before you go to write.

Interests and Activities: Topic-by-Topic Strategies

Here are a few of the most common overall areas that you may confront in terms of activities, interests, extracurriculars, and other pursuits. For now, we will focus on items directly related to college resumes and leave the more idiosyncratic interests to the side. (See Pages 73-77 for how to deal with those).

Local Community Service

Though a potentially strong topic—an excellent chance to demonstrate character and compassion—community service is not an entirely foolproof topic area.

Pros	Cons
Can demonstrate maturity and initiative	Can seem (by accident) condescending and pretentious
Heartwarming and lightly humorous episodes	Long explanations that merely repeat resume information
Communicates passion for and interest in everyday moments	Accidentally channels boredom, or seems entirely forced

There are a few common trends where local (as opposed to travel-oriented or international) community service essays are concerned. The first is that the best of these essays are rich with descriptive and narrative potential—so rich, in fact, that it is disheartening to ever see such potential go to waste. Consider a few forms of community service and the opportunities that they open.

- Tutoring and Mentoring ✓

Descriptions of quirky kids, equally (or more?) quirky supervisors, madcap adventures (try a sleep-away camp), and weirdly unforgettable settings (try, amazingly, a Kumon learning center)

- Work with Older People ✓

Life lessons, observations of stoicism and uplift (common in essays about hospitals and nursing homes), and enough humor to balance out the more serious notes (with the right topic, or with older people who have an endearing touch of Grampa Simpson in them)

- Work on a Project You Started ✓

Demonstration of initiative, adventures (and most likely some misadventures) in part-time entrepreneurship, satisfactions of making a vision into a reality

- Work with an Established Charity ✓

Demonstration of ability to work within a community, older and wiser (and often somewhat eccentric) charity colleagues, satisfying descriptions of finished projects that fit into a broader vision

Okay, so, how could any of this go wrong? In two gigantic ways, as you'll see on the next page.

If you are writing a community service essay, you must be especially careful of two overarching problems.

1) All Virtue, No Fun X

It is very hard to be intrinsically ill-inclined towards an essay that centers on the Wounded Warrior Project or Habitat for Humanity, or any similarly worthwhile humanitarian endeavor. But it is hard to be energized by such an essay on its own merits. To avoid sounding preachy, writers of community service essays require some cleverness, warmth, and idiosyncrasy. Without these ways of establishing approachability and, yes, of expressing a little fun, such essays can come off as haughty and moralistic even if that ISN'T the intention.

Remember, you're trying to get into a 21st-century college, not an 11th-century monastery.

2) All Information, No Interest X

Too often, students assume that the details and technicalities of a community service project will speak for themselves. This danger always arises for community service projects that students themselves devised, which after all exhibit great conscientiousness and independence. And this is NOT the case; NO amount of dry detail about dollars raised or families helped can replace a narrative that puts a human face on such efforts.

For this one, remember, you're reporting on scenes and incidents that mean something to you, not composing a 650-word business report.

Now, let's see the strengths and weaknesses of another common topic, athletics.

Athletics

Even if you are passionate about a sport, or about several sports, athletics-oriented topics involve unique assets and liabilities.

Pros	Cons
Builds upon your resume by showing, in new ways, why athletics is one of your most valued time commitments	Turns into a group of uninteresting technicalities, with few connections to your life and future beyond athletics
Individuals, scenes, and descriptions that are naturally memorable	Clichés about hard work and determination that readily undermine the essay
Can have a very lucid structure but lead into complex themes	Can have a hopelessly formulaic structure

Athletics will of course be prominent on many students' applications, but—considering the substantial "cons" column—you would be well-advised to see athletics as a VERY HIGH-RISK topic. Simply put, the clichéd version of athletics is becoming TOO COMMON. And that clichéd version goes something like this:

1) I love [INSERT SPORT]! X

2) I had a setback in [INSERT SPORT] and was [cut from the team/ injured/not sure I was good enough/whatever]! X

3) I worked really, really hard at [INSERT SPORT] because I am a hard worker! X

4) I had my hard work pay off and I love [INSERT SPORT] more than ever! X

Once you have gotten well past these clichés and dangers, you may nonetheless find that an athletics-based topic can work beautifully for your college essay. Try one of the following approaches.

- Your Community of Teammates ✔

Like many essay topics that revolve around social activity, athletics topics can automatically yield something like a "cast of characters." Coaches and team captains can be role models, of course, but can be just as interesting for their own quirks and flaws; you just need to know how to commit such complexity to paper.

- Your Unique Talents or Approach ✔

Did you develop a less-appreciated talent—like the ability to unfailingly avoid golf sandtraps—even in a well-known sport? Do the precise elements of the sport you play—tennis doubles as opposed to singles, for instance—say something about the rest of who you are as a person? If you find yourself gravitating to a small but significant detail of your life in athletics, an essay with such a focus may offer an outstanding chance to explain *why* that detail is so significant, no matter how small.

- Your Worldview as Formed by Athletics ✔

There is a good chance that the sports you play in high school will not DEFINE your college career, even if they remain hobbies or passions. Still, what lessons about teamwork can you take into the corporate world if you are an aspiring business major? What lessons about the value of constructive criticism can you take into the liberal arts if you gravitate to literature or philosophy? Sports are surprisingly effective at yielding broadly human insights.

Or did you choose another core topic? Read on for more pro-and-con breakdowns of acceptable essay content.

24

Are some sports better essay topics than others?

The answer here, as in so much of life: it's complicated. If you find yourself writing about a somewhat less expected sport (fencing or competitive figure skating, for example) as opposed to a more common one (basketball, baseball, soccer, etc.) you may have two natural advantages.

1) A less common sport may give you the ability to deliver especially vivid eye-opening descriptions. Many admissions readers have probably seen a game of baseball, but fewer have seen a game of competitive badminton—and if they have, such an obscure sport may still promise all sorts of unexpected instances.

2) Sports that are less common are ALSO sports that, in terms of recruitment if you are a competitive athlete, could put you at an advantage. If you are applying to a school that is looking for competitive rowers and you are a member of a crew team, consider using such athletic experience as your essay topic.

Unfortunately, an obscure sport is by NO MEANS automatically the key to a strong essay. Common sports may still offer much more insightful moments of human interest, and there is a downside to obscure sports: fake participation records for less common sports were part of the 2019 College Admissions Scandal. Colleges may now be skeptical of obscure athletics, so make sure that your passion for any sport that you discuss is both well-argued and sincere.

Cross-Cultural or International Identity

As with athletics, this one is a minefield of clichés. But as with athletics, this topic gives you the opportunity to confront issues of real consequence and themes of real depth—if you know the most obvious drawbacks.

Pros	Cons
Gives you the ability to exhibit versatility and adaptability	May seem heavy-handed and preachy without control of tone
Offers rich descriptions with the right level of self-reflection and attention to detail	Can have a strong early paragraph or two but lead into overly broad statements
Exhibits traits such as empathy, understanding, resourcefulness, and compromise	May require some political and social context, which may distract from personal traits

Extracurriculars in the Arts

This topic area encompasses a variety of activities, from individual portfolio projects to group- or outreach-based pursuits. Painting, sculpture, photography, acting, writing (including literary magazines, yearbooks, and newspapers), and music are all fair game here.

While there will be some constants with arts-based essays, the approach that you take can vary considerably depending on your specialty. An essay about idiosyncratic poetry or experimental film-making, for instance, may involve a primary emphasis on your own creative impulses. In almost complete contrast, an essay about an editorship or a leading role in the spring musical will demand some attention to collaboration or communication—almost as a sports essay would. Don't lose sight of such subtopic-by-subtopic subtleties, and don't forget that ANY arts topic you choose has pronounced pros and cons.

Pros	Cons
Celebrates a subject that American education, sadly, has come to prioritize less and less in the recent past	Needs to remain both heartfelt and personable, NOT to transform into a disapproving lecture
Offers a wealth of descriptive potential, even if your arts activities are mostly solitary	Threatens to become extremely cerebral without stark emotions or narrative episodes

Employment and Internships

For affecting and fast-paced narrative, employment experience can be perfect. Want humor? Realize that any workplace you've been in is, at some level, at LEAST as interesting as *The Office*'s own Dundler-Mifflin. Want something heartfelt? Take the life lessons of an older employee, a leader in your intended field, or an idealistic young co-worker, and commit those same lessons to print. Avoid a few common pitfalls and you will have an essay rich in the voices and perspectives of those you have worked alongside or worked for—to say nothing of your own point of view.

Pros	Cons
Situates your achievements in an adult context while offering potentially rich opportunities for description and dialogue	Requires vigilance to avoid predictability, since traits such as maturity are assumed for any conscientious applicant
Can provide a meaningful point of contact between your resume and your future intentions	May draw valid yet obvious or uninteresting linkages instead of bringing in new insights

If you have read this far, you should have an idea of the balance in terms of tone, theme, and message that you need to strike for some of the most reliably effective essay topics. It is now up to you to consider the other major aspect of the personal statement: your personality, as presented in the best possible light.

Character Traits:
Topic-by-Topic Strategies

Many students can succeed in settling on a basic positive quality: determination, intellectual drive, ambition, imagination. You would be surprised, though, how easy even qualities like THESE are to screw up. As it turns out, the reason behind such screw-ups is quite simple.

- *Every positive character trait is a cliché waiting to happen.*

Your task is to stay upbeat, to keep the emphasis on your good qualities, and to avoid clichés at any and all costs. The way you can do so is by keeping another unusual piece of personal statement reasoning in mind.

- *College essay students are often well aware of their positive traits, but NOT of what makes those traits unique or interesting.*

In short, will a student be aware that he or she is thoughtful, loyal, sociable? Yes. But aware of the highly individual spin that his or her life story puts on these commonly celebrated strengths of character? No, in many cases no.

To write an effective personal statement, you must be self-conscious in the best sense of the idea. Your traits are indeed admirable, but making the case that your version of endurance, cosmopolitanism, or community spirit is different from everyone else's will take extra effort and extra attention.

So let's see how, trait-by-trait.

Determination and Perseverance

Be warned: this one is often the kiss of death on sports topics, since it reduces them to an uninspired "passion + setback + improvement" formula. There are ways to handle the combination if your writing techniques are powerful enough, but why not see if this fits any unexpected combinations? Confronting writer's block, working an internship alongside genius software engineers, getting through to a special needs student—all of these are forms of perseverance and determination that an application reader will understand and value.

Pros	Cons
Common enough to bring together varied topics to form an interesting pattern	So common that it can become a toxic swamp of clichés if handled improperly
Can suggest other positive qualities easily (versatility, maturity, zen-like calm)	Can be hard to describe without obvious and corny "challenge" and "struggle" buzzwords

Intellectual Engagement

Isn't this one too obvious? After all, you're not thinking about college and possibly graduate school simply to watch lacrosse games and have a Chipotle in walking distance, now are you? Discussion of this theme is inevitable if your chosen essay topic relates to your major—for instance, if you are a longstanding member of a robotics club and want to major in electrical engineering or computer science anyway. But you will need to handle this one without an onslaught of vague phrases about "intellectual curiosity" and "a lifetime of learning" and "a passion for knowledge." Such phrasing can seek fake or pompous even if your passion for knowledge is genuine.

Here, the trick is to show rather than tell that you are fascinated with a topic. Love technology? Explain exactly what it is that intrigues you about car design, or aviation, or circuitry—the historical figures who sparked your interest, the gadgets and techniques that stun you with their elegance. The same goes for art, politics, medicine, *anything* that fires up your mind. Readers should feel that they are immersed in your world—that they are seeing your thoughts and passions as you see them—in every sentence.

Pros	Cons
Outstanding in both descriptive potential and possibilities for analysis, considering your expertise and commitment	Widely assumed as a reason for attending college in the first place and difficult to make a case for explaining at length
Can be applied to unexpected situations (see the "Costco Essay," Page 73) for original and surprisingly coherent results	Threat of being overwhelmed by broad and uninteresting phrases that may simply make a reader doubt your passion

Ambition, Entrepreneurship, Business Sense

In some situations, you may discuss your most pragmatic traits automatically—for instance, if you founded a club or have business-oriented extracurriculars. Still, the key to discussing practicality is to realize that it is NOT discipline-exclusive. Even an artist who loves obscure knowledge can be a shrewd operator. The trick, though, is to make sure that you strike a careful balance between practicality and humanity. Seem driven yet thoughtful, directed towards results yet eager to fulfill a meaningful purpose. Great improvements and genuine self-knowledge—not greed and gaudiness—motivate the best entrepreneurs.

Pros	Cons
Relevant to college coursework and thoughtful career planning regardless of actual major	Liable to result in an essay that is a "resume-dump" of awards and goals, not a narrative
Fascinating when used in "non-business" contexts	Possible to read as empty bragging when mis-handled

Altruism and Empathy

These qualities have apparent "best fit" topics—namely, volunteering and community service—but are more flexible than they might appear. Kindness and outreach can happen in family settings and in community activities that won't appear on a resume. Think about the last person you helped, make sure that the incident will turn out more like a Chekhov story than a *Lifetime* movie if you write it up, and see where these traits take you.

Pros	Cons
Powerful uses of perspective, dialogue, and detail	Potentially sentimental, making second opinions mandatory
Demonstrates purpose and a sense of conscience almost regardless of main topic	Threatens to eliminate any source of humor and quirkiness without proper handling

Here's a challenge: for the topic and trait that you have chosen, go back to the relevant pro-and-con lists and see (honestly) where your outlining or drafting so far fits. Pro, con, or in an uneasy middle region? If you don't trust your own judgment, have a trusted yet critical reader take a candid look. It may be possible to eliminate some brainstorming problems as you work on the drafts of your essay, but eliminating such problems at the outset is always preferable.

After all, as you will see in the next chapter, drafting is an art all its own. Make sure that your first principles are sound.

Part 2

Creating the
First Draft

Writing the Essay

How to Structure a Personal Statement

If you have worked through the last chapter, you already have much of the raw material that you will need to create an exceptional personal statement. Finding a structure for that material is your new challenge. Fortunately, it is a challenge that thousands of students in exactly your position have already conquered: this chapter takes the best of the methods that these applicants have used to write their essays—sentence-by-sentence and paragraph-by-paragraph—and presents you with a single versatile strategy.

First, though, a few ground rules.

1. *Every effective personal statement takes the form of a narrative and descriptive essay, NOT a five-paragraph argumentative essay, a standard expository essay, or anything of the sort.*

2. *The style should be poised yet conversational and spontaneous, NOT academic.*

3. *The essay can list some of your resume qualifications, but should NOT make them the sole focus.*

These three rules, especially the first, cannot be emphasized enough. Without keeping them in mind, you may wind up with an essay that has a logical structure and effective proofreading but that does nothing but harm your application.

To see what happens when these rules are broken, take a look at the essay excerpt on the opposite page. It is reasonably well structured and is completely free of errors; it is very close in voice and style to a term paper that would earn a high grade. But if you were to give essays like this to prestigious colleges, you would earn nothing but rejection after rejection.

There is a lot wrong with this essay, as the notes at the bottom explain, yet its cardinal sin is that it does not TELL THE WRITER'S STORY or REVEAL THE WRITER'S PERSONALITY. You will need to craft a narrative that actually engages your admissions readers, and that engagement must begin with the very first line.

Your Opening Sentence

The opening sentence of your personal statement should both

1. capture something essential about your personality and your narrative and
2. signal that you are writing a narrative, personal essay in the first place

While the first guideline given above is impossible to dispute—since your personal statement needs a unified theme, voice, and approach, after all—the second can seem a little . . . well, obvious? After all, who wouldn't write a personal opening for a personal statement?

As it turns out, LOTS of applicants. Unfortunately, plenty of students start out by writing personal statements that have the dry style of academic essays, or that ARE more or less academic essays with a few personal facts thrown in. You can't run the risk of giving your admissions readers something comparably bland and unexciting; in fact, you can't run the risk of letting them think, even for a second, that you are. The opening matters. A lot.

What happens when an essay starts off all wrong?

As far as the typical personal statement is concerned, "starting wrong" is mostly synonymous with "starting without a strong narrative." Of course, a writer can try a more analytic and distant approach to the topic.

That approach, though, will lose readers quickly. For instance, see when your interest in the excerpt below begins to evaporate.

The role of a medical professional is not simply to alleviate pain but to ensure quality of life in a way that extends beyond science. Often, once high-stakes lifesaving duties have subsided, it will be necessary to minister to those who have survived the struggle and whose needs demand a uniquely human touch. This is where one must shift from purely therapeutic measures to a larger number of human variables.

Duties of this sort are especially pronounced in the case of emergency medical technicians (EMTs). Normally, the on-the-job world of an EMT is fast-paced and high-stress. However, once the job is done, a practiced technician must assess best practices and prepare to learn from potentially unforeseen challenges. It is here that a psychological element of service during an emergency comes into play.

Now, the writer can try to build in a narrative later, but at that point the readers will probably have zoned out over the generalities about medicine. Why not build in true specificity and emotion immediately? Start with the material that makes the essay about YOU, then work towards broader significance.

Fortunately, there are a few standard personal statement openings that work quite well. And all of them, as you'll see below, use roughly the same strategy.

First Sentences That Work

In reading and analyzing literature, you might have encountered a plotting concept called "in medias res," which translates to "in the middle of things." The idea is that a story will more effectively engage its readers if it starts somewhere in the middle—with a dramatic, tense, or fascinating scene—and then backtracks to fill in information. Blockbuster movies use this concept to grip their audiences: start with an action scene, then fill in the viewers on who, exactly, all the characters are. You'll be using this concept almost regardless of what kind of opening sentence you choose.

Here are some opening sentences that pitch your reader right "into the middle of things" and are automatically engaging, when handled properly.

- A Scenic Detail ✔

Vivid and memorable descriptions that will both impress and intrigue the reader. EXAMPLE: *It's 5:30 on a Sunday, not a breeze to be felt; I'm watching a slim black model rocket, the first I had ever built, race into a blood-red sky.*

- A Fragment of Dialogue ✔

Short and meaningful exchanges that set a scene and generate suspense. EXAMPLE: *"That goose is the king!" shouted Matilda. Before I could stop her, she threw her Dora the Explorer backpack into the bushes and raced forward. "And I'm gonna catch him now!"*

- A Memorable Person ✔

Brief yet winning characterizations that capture fascinating personalities, and that subtly convey your own personality through sensitive description. EXAMPLE: *Fred Mercadante ran the campus ministry at St. Patrick's Church like a perpetual Dave Matthews Band concert. Bongos, guitars, impromptu tents, and Fred presiding over it all in John Lennon glasses and a bandanna— each meeting we had was like an alt-rock masterpiece.*

- A Moment of Tension ✔

Evocations of uncertainty or conflict that will prompt the reader to continue on in search of resolution. EXAMPLE: *For two seconds, the whole world halted. Then time re-started, and I was faced with a deafening silence and 50 cartons of broken eggs.*

Those are the ones that work, and that work beautifully. Now, let's talk about the opening sentences that typically DON'T work—and which themselves fail for related reasons.

Sentences That Mostly DO NOT Work

You may have noticed that effective personal statement openings are nothing like the essay openings that are taught in many high school and even college courses. This difference should not be entirely surprising: remember, you MUST differentiate your personal statement from an academic essay in the most efficient and intelligent manner possible.

But even then, is it acceptable to adapt one of the standard academic essay openings—for instance, a question, a definition, a general claim, or a quotation from an authority—to the personal statement?

Alas, no, frequently it is not. To see why—to see what these self-destructing openings share, and to further clarify why openings that work do work—consider each of these types on its own.

- A Question $\boxed{X}$

These tend to be so vague and generic (example: "People always asked me, 'What do you want to be when you grow up?'") that they quickly backfire. Sometimes they simply call attention to themes from the prompt (example: "Have you ever faced a challenge that made you doubt yourself?") in a truly cringe-worthy manner.

- A Definition $\boxed{X}$

Like questions, many of these are on-theme, simplistic, and wholly unimpressive. Do NOT define "courage," "perseverance," or any other broad trait, and do not cite the Merriam-Webster dictionary as though it is somehow an impressive source here. It isn't.

- A General Claim $\boxed{X}$

Vague and unhelpful beyond explaining the topic or thesis, general claims may have a place ELSEWHERE in the essay. But starting with a statement like "I thrive on intellectual curiosity" or "I have never been afraid of obstacles" doesn't do anything to show the reader what is unique about your experience. It doesn't help that the phrases themselves will strike many readers as trite.

- A Quotation $\boxed{X}$

The essay is about you, NOT about Gandhi or Michelle Obama. Even if you do find a relevant quote, chances are that 1) it will throw off the structure of your opening and 2) it will read like you Googled "quotes about [insert quality]" and picked the first one.

So what do these undesirable openings have in common?

1. At best, they awkwardly communicate themes that would be MUCH BETTER communicated using the openings that do work.

2. At worst, they introduce statements so obvious, cliché, or pointless that the ENTIRE essay may suffer where your admissions reader is concerned.

Yet as with many elements of putting together a personal statement, there are times when even the unacceptable openings, miraculously, become acceptable. These instances are rare, but are worth a little investigation nonetheless.

What If You Have a Great "Unacceptable" Opening?

Welcome to the Twilight Zone, Bizarro World, the Dark Side—or the closest that your typical college essay opening has to any of those things. If you're reading this section closely, chances are that you are determined to pick apart the rules that this book has given you, or are hell-bent on taking a risk. Rule-questioning and risk-taking are two personality traits that, after all, can yield incredibly powerful college essays.

This section, however, comes with one major warning: before you can BREAK the rules of a college essay, you must MASTER the rules that normally work. In other words, if you do break one of the rules given earlier, you need to do so in a way that improves upon personal statement strategies that have already been proven to work.

So use a great "unacceptable" opening only after reflection and with a tactical sensibility. Any opening that assumes a typically weak format will need to compensate in some form, usually in terms of content according to the following rule.

- **Fascinating content can OVERCOME liabilities in an otherwise weak (question, definition, general claim, quotation) opening format.**

However, this premise raises a loaded question: exactly how fascinating does your content need to be in order to nullify the typical format-based weaknesses? Answer: immensely so. Here are a few opening sentences that would ACTUALLY work despite typically weak structures.

- Interesting Questions ✔

- Do octopuses see precisely the same colors that we do? Do nocturnal tapirs? Do horseshoe crabs?
- Can you ever be too obsessive about furniture design?
- Is it *really* possible to program a computer to beat the stock market every hour, every day, every minute?

- Interesting Definitions ✔

- Success, as I see it, is three potential investors muttering "this is nuts . . . " and the fourth one shouting "here's $150,000!"
- There are many forms of courage: getting up at 5:30 A.M. to memorize pluperfect Latin verbs is, amazingly, the form I prefer.
- For a good cook, "failure" means that everyone at the table mutters "um, this is nice, thanks" and starts sprinkling on the garlic salt and the pepper flakes at the first opportunity.

- Interesting General Claims ✔

- Orchids are the world's most bipolar plants.
- Watching a bridge collapse is exactly as terrifying as it sounds.
- Unless you have an appetite for both madness and adventure, never try to use an ATM in Paris after 11:00 at night.

42

- Interesting Quotations ✔

- "The fascist octopus has sung its swan song." - George Orwell (essay about learning from slips of the tongue in debate)
- "To be fond of dancing was a certain step towards falling in love." - Jane Austen (essay about frequenting a tango and milonga studio);
- "If two wrongs don't make a right, how many wrongs do?" - Clara B., age 10 (essay about working with an after-school program in a low-income neighborhood)

Note that, in addition to simply being intriguing and surprising, these first sentences DEFINITELY hint at narrative content. They are both personalized and connected to the rest of the essay in a manner that a quote about "change" from John F. Kennedy, a definition of "leadership," or a question about "facing challenges" never will be.

The Core Essay Structure

Any reader will need to see, without much difficulty, what your life story is about and what you are trying to communicate about your strengths of character. So, structure-wise, what will a solid personal statement look like? For the sake of clarity, you can divide up the tasks of narrative and analysis using the essay format that follows.

1) It will be roughly FOUR paragraphs long if you keep each segment consolidated

2) It will break down into TWO main segments (first and third) that mostly narrative detail and TWO other key segments (second and fourth) that are mostly analysis and summation

3) It will NEVER involve a paragraph that is completely general or free of details

Why this format? Well, at roughly 650 words maximum, a personal statement gives you room for roughly four decently-sized (or 150- to 200-word) paragraphs or (more likely) multi-paragraph stages of prose. You need to show that you can present, develop, and close out a coherent thought. Moreover, you need to show that you can work both with precise details and with the big picture: the two-two format described above will automatically keep your essay from feeling monotonous.

Of course, if by now you know what shape your essay should take, by all means, start writing. It is possible that you have worked through your ideas, that you know how they are connected, and that most of what need to do is "get it all on paper" and then edit away. If that's your case, you might jump ahead to the Editing the Essay content that constitutes Chapter 3. The problem is that, realistically, most students are not equipped to write the full essay on the fly: even if you have seen example after example of personal statement prowess, how it is all PUT TOGETHER can still be supremely elusive.

Here is how to build the best possible personal statement, piece by piece, paragraph by paragraph.

Rules of Structure: Specific to General, and Back Again

In order to create an essay that shows variety and versatility, you will need to move effectively from precise, vivid details to broader, consequential analysis of what all those details mean. To see how this format plays out, consider some excerpts from a well-crafted essay about the sense of community that a student discovered on his school swim team. The essay itself is available in its entirety on Pages 111-113.

STEP 1: The essay begins with a narrative scenario that is meant to keep the reader moving forward—"It's 5:30 in the morning on a Saturday, and all fourteen of us should be in bed." Why are "all fourteen of us" up so early, and who are "all fourteen of us" anyway? The essay should answer these questions while providing further narrative details and establishing its core themes.

STEP 2: After providing a description of an episode from his life on the swim team, the writer transitions to broader analysis of his commitment to swimming—"It's no secret that I'm not the world's greatest swimmer: if you were five-five with a minor heart condition, would you be trying to be the next Michael Phelps?" The essay is shifting to a more direct discussion of team-based friendships. Still, the writing is detailed and personable, not dry and needlessly high-minded.

STEP 3: The essay shifts back to a scene, but a DIFFERENT one than in the beginning—"I've just finished my fourth and last race of the meet." Such a time jump is perfectly appropriate, so long as the writer keeps the essay centered on a clear set of admirable character traits.

STEP 4: As the essay winds down, the writer introduces broad-based final thoughts—"We may wonder if close connection is possible today; technology, the argument goes, has been more successful in driving people apart than in bringing them together." Note that such a widely-applicable statement would NOT have been appropriate earlier. It is appropriate here, though, because the writer has already demonstrated a talent for specificity and has determined how to connect overarching ideas about society to a vivid personal narrative.

Rules of Structure: Transitions

If you are accustomed to using rather blatant transitions, please, get un-accustomed to them. One of the WORST things you can do in a personal statement is to link paragraphs with sentence-opening transitions such as "First . . . Next . . . Finally" (which are simply childish) or "To begin . . . Moreover . . . Furthermore" (which— seriously, what human being talks like this? a cartoon butler?).

Instead, you will need to create transitions that are supremely subtle: they will still be there to guide and order the prose, but they will not stick out in any distracting or amateurish way.

Try this: set up your paragraphs so that the ideas flow logically one into the next WITHOUT the use of any especially obvious transitions. Then, as needed, bring in transitions that would occur in conversation. A well-placed "though" or "in fact" or "that said" can give clarity to how your thoughts move along, whether placed at the beginning of a sentence or (as occurs in conversation somewhat more than in essay writing) towards the end or middle.

Rules of Structure: Mini-Paragraphs

To keep the essay conversational, and to create moments of high emphasis, one- or two-sentence paragraphs aren't simply allowed. They're RECOMMENDED. Of course, using paragraphs that register at this length is a departure from the conventions of most analytic essays. Yet a sentence, phrase, or even word that is loaded with meaning should be made to stand out.

The trick, though, is that you do not want to become over-reliant on extremely short and emphatic paragraphs. Such dependence has drawbacks—including the prospect of a choppy and seemingly disconnected structure. You don't want to leave the reader with any doubts (whether fair or not) about whether you can sustain longer, more complex thoughts

Here's a way to strike a balance: choose only THREE ideas for mini-paragraphs and make sure that these ideas are central to the theme of your essay. In this way, you will create mini-paragraphs that justify their existence and that balance out your longer portions of discussion.

Also, keep the following exception in mind, since not all short paragraphs properly fall under the mini-paragraph heading.

- ***Dialogue should NORMALLY be formatted so that each new speaker is given a new paragraph.***

To see how dialogue formatting works, consult the sample essay on Pages 111-113. But to see how TRUE mini-paragraphs work, consult the sample essay on Page 105-117, which avoids dialogue in favor of concise points that reflect the author's line of thinking.

Three Alternative Structures

If you find that you do not gravitate to the essential structure given above, fear not! There are other options, but understanding them and working with them well require a firm sense of how to take specific information about events in your life and combine it with more general information about the traits that define you.

Unified Flow

It is entirely possible that—with the standard rules about topic, theme, and narrative detail well in mind—you can begin writing and simply see where the essay takes you. This is a route that is only recommended under two conditions, though.

1. You have brainstormed so aggressively that the essay takes shape without too much systematic thought about structure.

2. You are a practiced creative writer and can work with narrative or description in extremely short bursts.

Working with this one is a matter of both inspiration and background. The sample essay on Pages 105-107 offers a successful demonstration of this loose structure—quick action and little dialogue, but a flow of consistently vivid descriptions and reflections.

Triple-Shot Narrative

Consider this scenario: you have a personal quality and a few topics or timeframes that you see as compelling material, but are NOT sure that the Core Structure or a Unified Flow would work. There is an alternative. Simply "frame" a few different episodes and explain how (or subtly suggest how) they connect.

This Triple-Shot Structure is one of the best ways to handle time jumps. The trick, though, is that your introduction and conclusion must provide context without becoming so general that they fail to engage your readers. For instance, how might you frame the following three episodes in an essay about competitive gymnastics?

Episode 1: The writer remembers the thrill of navigating an inflatable obstacle course as a very young child.

Episode 2: The writer perfected her ability to do back handsprings in the fourth grade.

Episode 3: The writer prepared for an important gymnastics meet despite lingering self-doubts.

Here are some topic possibilities for the opening and closing, which should return to the SAME point in order to effectively "frame" the writer's other ideas and memories.

1. A significant detail or symbol that the writer noticed

2. An event close in time to the writer's present, in order to put the episodes in perspective

3. A series of reflections (IF they are original enough) on the core quality that the episodes demonstrate

In short, the main Triple-Shot structure will normally be "introduction . . . three distinct episodes . . . conclusion." There are possible tweaks, though. In particular, you can eliminate EITHER the introduction or conclusion if you feel that the themes are evident enough and that the essay takes on a unified shape with fewer main segments. Note, though, that you cannot eliminate both. Some context and reflection must be present for a reader—particularly a quick reader—to understand how your episodes add up.

Specific-General-Specific

Some students have trouble writing conclusions that, while remaining on-topic, actually add something 1) new and 2) interesting to the essay. Without additional, engaging information or reflections of this sort, a conclusion becomes little more than redundant dead weight. The answer? If you feel that you cannot pull off a traditional conclusion that clinches the essay in an assertive and energetic manner, simply go back to the narrative.

Admittedly, there are dangers to this approach. In order to sacrifice a traditional conclusion, you MUST make sure that your main ideas are fully apparent on the basis of the narrative itself.

There are, though, some essays that benefit from this structure, particularly essays that address significant challenges and changes of character. You might be able to pull off a structure that centers on two "snapshot" narratives—one that opens the essay, another that closes it. In between, you will need to set up a section of character analysis that anticipates your second narrative and establishes the meaning or message behind your experience.

Now that you have everything you need to write a first draft, you are welcome to get to work. And once that first draft is ready, set it aside. The next stage of writing your personal statement is a matter of using your time wisely and making useful changes gradually; reflection and honest self-assessment, here, are essential.

Part 3

Reviewing, Revising, and Refining

Editing to Impress

Uses of Revisions and Second Opinions

Effective revision for college application essays is partially a matter of traditional line editing, partially a matter of making sure that your words have the right kind of impact on your readers. For this chapter, the two areas will be treated separately. In most cases, you should begin with grammar and proofreading, then move on to matters of audience response.

Still, there are exceptions to that "in most cases" protocol. Consider starting with reader reactions if you are writing a high-risk essay topic, are not sure that you have done your topic justice, or have not done much narrative writing in the past. In this way, you will either build your confidence or shut down a potentially troublesome essay BEFORE committing time to proofreading.

Also: if your time to write a personal statement is limited, first impressions should be gathered sooner rather than later. Again, investing in an essay that could backfire, deleting a draft or two, and learning from that experience is not always worth it time-wise.

Proofreading, though, is a somewhat more technical and mechanical stage of the process. To keep you working with grammar rules that may be familiar from analytic essays, this chapter begins with straightforward editing standards.

Proofreading and Grammar

The guidelines that are emphasized here are, for the most part, dedicated to grammar errors that go BEYOND a basic spellcheck or grammar check. Even the better proofreading programs (such as Grammarly) may not detect some of the editing flaws that you will find below.

Pronoun Agreement

Flaws in pronoun use come in a few forms. Watch, to begin, for confusions involving "IT" and "THEY."

"It" Usage

- Singular and CANNOT refer to a person

- Used to refer back to group-related nouns ("committee," "college," "government," "group") that are grammatically singular

It will always be wrong, for instance, to use the following constructions

> Early in one of Virginia Woolf's essays, it states . . . **X**
> (since a person must "state")

> Yet my team summoned their energies . . . **X**
> (since "team" is singular)

However, the following versions feature proper usage (or avoidance) of "it."

> Early in one essay, Virgina Woolf states . . . ✔

> Yet my team summoned its energies . . . ✔

The Proofreading Checklist

Does your essay successfully meet the following criteria in terms of writing style?

_____ Relatively advanced but not showy vocabulary

_____ Variety of sentence structures and openings

_____ Differences in sentence length and punctuation

_____ Proper transitions from idea to idea

_____ NO spelling or punctuation errors that would be easily caught with a program like Grammarly

---

If you have time, check through the essay to see if you have avoided the following more obscure grammar problems. Some are covered in this book; others are addressed at length in the PrepVantage SAT series.

_____ No misplaced modifiers or unclear pronouns

_____ No pronoun or possessive pronoun problems ("it" vs "they", "its" vs "it's", etc.)

_____ Proper uses of semicolons, colons, and dashes

_____ Proper uses of words for countable items (number, many, fewer) and non-countable quantities (amount, much, less)

"They" Usage

- Plural and CAN refer to either persons or things

- CANNOT be used to refer to collective nouns (as noted above) that should take "it" instead, or to tricky SINGULAR pronouns ("everyone," "nobody," "somebody," "either," "neither") that should technically take versions of "he" or "she"

In addition to avoiding "they" for certain collective yet singular nouns ("group," "assembly," "corporation," etc.), you must avoid using "they" to refer to ANY singular individual. This can be a tricky rule because it is frequently over-looked in everyday speech.

> . . . of course, since the **coach** for the other team did everything **they** could to enable **their** players to succeed . . . **X** ("they" and "their" wrongly refer to "coach," singular)

Don't breeze past errors such as these. Just know that a SINGULAR person can only take "his" or "her" references, and that "coach" should take the one of these possessives. If you are uncomfortable with rules such as these, you may also try for entirely new constructions that avoid tricky pronoun references.

> . . . of course, since the **coach** for the other team did everything **she** could to enable **her** players to succeed . . . (corrects the sentence by creating a singular reference back to "coach") ✔

> . . . of course, the players found that their coach did everything possible to help the team succeed . . . (avoids the pronoun construction but STILL delivers a clear idea and preserves the main themes) ✔

56

Misplaced Modifier

Misplaced modifier errors are easy to read past UNLESS you pay close attention to references and alignment. For instance, an inattentive reader may not notice that there is anything wrong with the following sentence.

> Like any competitive weightlifter, new challenges will always arise despite my best efforts.

Apparently, the sentence explains that the writer is a competitive weightlifter who faces "new challenges"—but this is NOT how the grammar of the sentence lines up. Instead, the phrase "Like any competitive weightlifter" wrongly describes the challenges faced by the writer, NOT the writer himself or herself. This is a standard misplaced modifier error: all the necessary words are technically in the sentence, but the ordering (describing a challenge as a weightlifter) reduces the sentence to nonsense.

To detect misplaced modifier, simply prioritize the following question as you read.

- *Do descriptive phrases (particularly longer ones) line up with the logically correct nouns?*

In this case, you need to pair off the description with a noun that references a person. Thus, the following version is both logically and grammatically correct.

> Like any **competitive weightlifter, I** will always face new challenges despite my best efforts. ✔

Still, how big of a problem is an error like misplaced modifier? True, it is not too dangerous to lapse into one or two subtle errors of this sort. If you are coordinating several descriptions, though, they must be crisp, logical, and able to pass a perceptive admissions reader.

Avoiding Comma Splices

A comma splice involves combining two independent clauses with ONLY a comma—a unit of punctuation that on its own cannot perform this function. Keep in mind that a single sentence must contain ONLY ONE INDEPENDENT CLAUSE and make sure to avoid problems such as the following.

> At first, none of the traditional lesson plans engaged the class, I soon discovered that a more experimental approach held promise. **X** (NOTE: multiple independent clauses - 1. "none . . . engaged" 2. "I . . . discovered")

There are a few different strategies for correcting comma splices. One is to insert a transition or conjunction that can turn an independent clause into a subordinate clause. The word "although" could offer an appropriate transition if inserted before the word "I" in the example above, yet there are other possibilities. Some appropriate words here are commonly known as FANBOYS (or coordinating) conjunctions and include the following items.

FANBOYS: **F**OR   **A**ND   **N**OR   **B**UT   **O**R   **Y**ET   **S**O

Other words can serve similar functions in creating dependent or subordinate clauses: "because," "since," "while," and (as already noted) "although" are some of the most common. However, it is also possible to correct a comma splice by creating MULTIPLE sentences and by inserting transition words that do NOT affect the fundamental structure of a sentence. Both of the forms that follow are appropriate.

- At first, none of the traditional lesson plans engaged the **class, yet** I soon discovered that a more experimental approach held promise. ✔

What about sentence fragments? How acceptable are they?

If you have been studying for the ACT or the SAT in the recent past, you have probably been taught to avoid sentence fragments—non-grammatical units of speech that do not feature a proper main subject, a proper main verb, or both. But why hasn't this book stressed sentence fragments so far? The answer: they actually ARE acceptable on the college essay under two conditions.

1. The purpose is to deliver quick DETAILS or to generate a strong DRAMATIC EFFECT.

2. The same vivid expression would NOT normally call for a proper subject-verb construction.

For a demonstration of the first condition, see the opening of the sample essay on Pages 105-107. Here, fragments are used strategically, in a listing of details that both sets a scene and establishes the writer's voice.

Nonetheless, fragments ARE a problem if they occur in a manner that is more clearly accidental. An explanatory or analytic sentence that runs somewhat long, for instance, and does NOT have a proper main clause should not be treated as a fragment. Unless a reader can clearly see that fragments are for expressive purposes, avoid fragments.

In any case, use fragments sparingly. They should reinforce key points, NOT prop up a whole essay.

- At first, none of the traditional lesson plans engaged the **class. However,** I soon discovered that a more experimental approach held promise. ✔

The second of these forms, which employs two separate sentences and the transition "However," can also be written using a different punctuation and capitalization convention—if you are familiar with semicolon usage. A semicolon will typically function like a period WITHOUT capitalization and can thus resolve a comma splice.

- At first, none of the traditional lesson plans engaged the **class; however,** I soon discovered that a more experimental approach held promise. ✔

Refining Sentence Structure

To make sure that you have an effective, varied, and mature style sentence-by-sentence, you should keep the following rules in mind.

1) Vary Sentence Openings

To make sure that your writing style is not monotonous, make sure that you vary the way you begin your sentences. A good rule to follow is the following.

- Just over HALF of your sentences should feature simple declarative sentence or independent clause openings ("I will never forget that . . ."; "Dr. Mulvey raced down the hall . . .")

- Just under HALF of your sentences should open with transitions ("In contrast, . . ."; "Still, . . .") or subordinate clauses ("Although that wasn't the only time . . ."; "Because such luck is rare . . .")

This variety is not hard to achieve, and is the first step towards creating impressively varied sentence structure overall. Moreover, repeated openings stand out for the worst reasons, as in the following example.

> I trudged through the snow. I finally knew what Jack London was getting at in "To Build a Fire." My nose was running. My feet were sore. My family might as well have been a million miles away. My boots were full of icy slush, and with each step I realized that my judgment—try one of the tougher slopes on a first skiing trip—couldn't possibly have been worse.

The sentences are grammatically correct, but all open with simplistic-sounding noun-verb phrases. Try for more variety.

> As I trudged through the snow, I finally knew what Jack London was getting at in "To Build a Fire." My nose was running; my feet were sore. At that point, my family might as well have been a million miles away. With each step of my slush-filled boots, I realized that my judgment—try one of the tougher slopes on a first skiing trip—couldn't possibly have been worse.

The changes are minimal, but the style has lost its repetitive quality.

2) Vary Sentence Length

Problems with sentence length are harder to spot on the fly than problems with sentence openings. But you can start to improve your style in this respect by keeping the following guideline in mind.

- OVERALL, you want a BALANCE of relatively short (independent clause, possibly short transitions) sentences and relatively long (subordinate clauses, complex prepositional phrases, lists) sentences

61

It is somewhat difficult to find a rule of proportions here. However, if sentence length is a problem in your essays, you can figure out how to improve your style based on your particular weaknesses.

Too Many Long Sentences

- Break up run-ons

- Add relevant short sentences for impact

Consider the following portion of a descriptive paragraph, which crams too much information into one long and awkward sentence.

> *"Can you help me Mister Robot-o?"* I sang in my best tin man voice as I pumped my arms up and down and mechanically swiveled my head from side to side, trying to forget that I was armored in hockey pads and pieces of Xerox boxes—all spray-painted silver—and dancing myself senseless at a county fair in the middle of a 90-degree day in June.

The grammar is technically correct, but the author's ideas appear to be thrown together—and will certainly be hard for a quick reader to sort out. Break up this sentence while achieving a diversity of sentence lengths and structures.

> *"Can you help me Mister Robot-o?"* I sang in my best tin man voice. Then I pumped my arms up and down and mechanically swiveled my head from side to side. Armored in hockey pads and pieces of Xerox boxes—all spray-painted silver—I was dancing myself senseless at a county fair in the middle of a 90-degree day in June.

Too Many Short Sentences

Here is a paragraph that does not feature any clear grammatical problems, even though the writing has other clear technical flaws.

> Each book is different. Some are aggressively dog-eared. Others are so pristine they might never have been read. Some are bound in tough burgundy leather. Others are floppy paperbacks. Each one, though, has shaped me. I have refined my attention to detail with each art catalog. I have harnessed my love of adventure with each Y.A. novel. Every book here matters.

To improve the flow of the writing, use the following guidelines.

• Combine judiciously while checking for grammar

• Check for structure and create better transitions

Sequences of short sentences are somewhat easier to catch: such portions often make for choppy reading and often (as an added weakness) feature phrases that follow extremely similar structures. Again, the grammar is mostly correct, but the sentence construction shows little skill in combining and connecting ideas. Just follow the combination and transition rules outlined above.

> Each book is different: some are aggressively dog-eared, whole others are so pristine they might never have been read. Some are bound in tough burgundy leather. Others are floppy paperbacks. Still, each one has shaped me. From art catalogs that refined my attention to detail to Y.A. novels that spurred my love of adventure, every book here matters.

Also, keep in mind that barrages of short sentences are NOT ENTIRELY BAD at an early drafting stage. If you need to simply get your ideas on the page, use short sentences to do so. Once you begin the later essay editing stages, though, you must do more to make sure that your ideas are both clear (as they may be in super-short sentences) and elegantly connected.

Your Audience: Second Opinions

After all that work with grammar, here is the portion of the editing process that frequently matters most of all. Grammatical mastery will of course save you time and energy. You won't need to expend your attention on English usage mistakes if you have taken this chapter to heart before moving on to the supplemental essays, for instance. With such aptitude, you can shift your emphasis from rote proofreading to the high-stakes matter of how, exactly, your audience will respond to your work.

And audience reception is a VERY high-stakes issue. There is an unfortunate off-chance that—even if you have followed all of the guidelines laid out in this book—your essay will run into problems. You may assume a pretentious or haughty tone (without realizing that you are doing so). You may have narrative episodes that are well-described but off-topic (without ever identifying them as problematic). And you may—as even the best writers sometimes do—write an essay that makes sense from your own perspective but that confuses or confounds outside readers.

For these reasons and more, you should take ANY finished essay that you have and ask a reader to assess it according to the checklist on the opposite page. Stress that you need an honest assessment, NOT a polite one. Because the "Second Opinion Checklist" can be such a sensitive manner, a Question-and-Answer segment for how to use this portion of the book can be found on the next few pages.

The Second Opinion Checklist

Find a reader who will give you honest responses to the following questions, then ask him or her to complete this questionnaire.

- How many vivid and impressive descriptions or details did you find in this essay? UNDERLINE them in the draft, add up, and choose from below.

0-3 (awful)   4-8 (decent)   9 or more (awesome)

* * *

How many times did you do the following while reading the essay?

laugh: ____   cheer: ____   feel enlightened: ____

If the total number of times for these three actions is lower than 5, the essay MUST be revised.

* * *

- In one sentence, what is the message of this essay?
  _____
  _____

- In one sentence, what sets this applicant apart from other applicants with _____ as a topic and _____ as a main character trait?
  _____
  _____

If you cannot quickly provide a single clear sentence for either question, the essay MUST be revised.

QUESTION: Whom should I ask to review my essay?

ANSWER: An English or writing teacher, an experienced tutor, a friend or sibling with high-profile acceptances—ANYONE who will be HONEST and WELL-INFORMED.

REASONING: You want to run the essay by readers who 1) know something about how to tell an engaging story and who 2) have a track record that you can trust. The people mentioned above would, on average, stand pretty good chances of fitting these criteria. These people would also know that being less than honest about your writing comes at a cost. What would you rather have—a few drafts that you're told to delete, or a bunch of rejection letters?

QUESTION: Should I ask a parent or a guidance counselor?

ANSWER: Frequently, NO, or ONLY as a LAST RESORT.

REASONING: Consider this reality: how many times have your parents or your guidance counselor successfully directed students to top-level acceptances? If the answer is "almost always," by all means, enlist these individuals for editing and feedback.

Otherwise, consider the dangers. Some guidance counselors do NOT work exclusively with competitive applications and may, thus, be uninformed or overly lenient in terms of an essay's true weaknesses. Parents also have a bad tendency to foist their own ideas on applicants. They know what they like and admire about you, but do your mother and father know how to craft a high-stakes application essay for complete strangers? Possibly not.

QUESTION: How honest should my readers be?

ANSWER: As honest as humanly possible, including quick first impressions. If need be, absolutely merciless.

REASONING: There is no guarantee that an admissions reader will be hospitable towards an essay with perceptible flaws. Even notoriously subjective matters such as "likability" have been used by admissions committees (as a 2018 lawsuit against Harvard University revealed). For these reasons, you need to have readers criticize your essay from as many standpoints as possible—including a few that would appear to be unfair in a perfect world.

QUESTION: Some of the goals on the checklist—laughter, wisdom, stunning descriptions—seem beyond me. Can I write an essay of this quality even if I'm not a practiced creative writer?

ANSWER: Absolutely.

REASONING: This is one essay and, if you bought this book far enough in advance, you have months at your disposal to get it right. You may not be a practiced creative writer. However, you HAVE had experiences that are moving, hilarious, or rich in insight—and if you haven't, then you've been doing high school all wrong. Get those experiences on the page, THEN worry about writing technique and reader reception as you refine.

There is one other reason to be so aggressive about second opinions: sometimes, taking a risk on the essay is necessary. But how do you manage riskier topics and formats from the outset, BEFORE taking a risk that is ultimately unwise? Discover how in the next chapter.

Part 4

How to Break the Rules

Offbeat Essays
Getting Odd, and Staying Meaningful

Part 1: Breaking the Topics

First off, there are times when a topic that seems ready to self-destruct can give you a bulletproof essay. But to see how this can happen, you can't rely too much on abstract ideas, at least not at first. Instead, you need to see the up-close difference between the self-destructing version and the bulletproof version, which are designed using very different principles.

So, take a look at one of the essay topics that is normally guaranteed to bore an admissions reader into oblivion: Being Undecided. Start by reading this essay opening, which is how the Being Undecided topic plays out most of the time.

> Throughout my life, I have alwas been drawn to a plethora of academic disciplines. Because I value knowledge that is diverse, I find it difficult to make a single commitment that would define my intellectual life in college. The question "What do you want to study?" is thus a question that I find uniquely difficult; I find myself still "undecided" but eager to learn all I can.

As you can see if you have taken this book's guidelines to heart, there is plenty wrong with this personal statement, including

- Seemingly endless repetitions of similar ideas

- Lack of meaningful or interesting details

- No sources of human interest in terms of dialogue or conflict

- Nothing interesting or unique about the writer's personality

The problem, in short, is that there is nothing that appeals to or impresses an admissions reader. Remember, readers need to be won over in terms of both WRITING STYLE and APPLICANT PERSONALITY, and this essay wins in neither category.

Frankly, essays that break away from acceptable topics need to compensate in BOTH of these areas. What would such compensation for an essay topic as typically over-used and under-whelming as Being Undecided look like? Well, like the following essay opening.

> The auditorium fell quiet. A few moments, and the stage was lit up with filaments of green, bulbs of purple, sparks of blue. I was mesmerized, enthralled—and, as an 7-year-old at the Liberty Science Center laster lights show, confused. Was it art? Science? Entertainment? A dream?
>
> I couldn't decide then, and can't now. But the truth is that I thrive on glorious indeterminacy.

Now, consider what this essay opening does right. It has 1) a clear narrative source of interest, 2) a meaningful and personable approach to the theme, and 3) details that are crisp, vivid, and significant.

In short, in order to make ANY topic that is normally off-limits even come close to working, you need traditional forms of excellence.

72

It's worth remembering, though, that there are some topics that are so problematic that no amount of narrative and descriptive talent can salvage them. These are listed in detail on Pages 8-11. Keep in mind that off-limits topics are typically rife with hopeless clichés, likely to make a reader question your judgment, or both.

Still, there is an entire swath of topics that this book has not yet explored in any fundamental way. Read on, and discover how the elements of your personality that have NOT been discussed at length—your most personal quirks—can actually provide the foundation for an entire college application essay.

The Quirk-Based Essay

On the face of it, which of these would make a better personal statement topic?

1. Practicing relentlessly to become an outstanding cross-country runner

2. Shopping at Costco

The question of which topic is superior depends on the classic idea that some things are better in theory than in practice. Still, it is completely understandable if the "Shopping at Costco" topic has you shaking your head and wondering "what on Earth are these people thinking? Costco?"

In Theory

If you picked Topic 1, you have made a reasonable choice: this is a significant topic (cross-country) that demonstrates character (determination). As for Topic 2, Costco, Costco? What admissions officer at Dartmouth or UNC or Stanford, or anywhere but a college for rodeo clowns, wants to read about Costco?

In practice, though, the situation couldn't be more different.

In Practice

Here, if you picked Topic 1, you have picked a topic that routinely produces essays so bland that they are almost unbearable. It is possible to write a fantastic essay about cross-country running, especially if the descriptions and personal reflections are intense and thoughtful. More often, though, the "determination in cross-country" topic reduces itself to a series of platitudes about "hard work" and "believing in myself" and "the sacrifice was worth it"— to an essay with an unoriginal theme and few details that anyone, anywhere, would see as remarkable.

But this time, if you picked Topic 2, you have picked a topic that got a student named Brittany Stinson into Stanford, not to mention "Yale, Columbia, University of Pennsylvania, Dartmouth, and Cornell" in 2016. (Read more at https://www.businessinsider.com/high-school-senior-who-got-into-5-ivy-league-schools-shares-her-admissions-essay-2016-4.) Costco did all that. And Papa John's can do almost as much; one year later, a student named Carolina Williams wrote an essay about ordering pizza that got her into Yale. (Read more at https://www.businessinsider.com/papa-johns-essay-helps-high-school-senior-get-into-yale-2017-5.) Hands-down, Topic 2 is the better practical choice. But how?

Why, and How, Quirky Topics Work

The array of "quirky topics" is virtually endless. Playing an old Sega Genesis, setting up an above-ground pool, re-arranging a refrigerator so that the items are grouped by color—the list can begin here and go on indefinitely. However, even these topics must be chosen with care, for one simple reason.

- *Quirky topics DO NOT work SIMPLY because they are quirky.*

Choosing a quirky topic is not a guarantee of success; it may give you a way of standing out from the pile of applicants, but there is no guarantee that it will give you a route to an acceptance letter. Yet the advantage of being noticed for something offbeat and intriguingly counterintuitive—Costco, Costco!—cannot be denied. Once your personal statement has been noticed, it is up to you to put your quirks to good use.

Indeed, quirky topics WORK because they

1. Start by grabbing attention

2. Continue by laying out your meaningful positive qualities

3. Succeed THROUGHOUT in drawing the reader into your world

In other words, a quirky topic functions more like a "significant" topic than you might think. You are still creating a vision of yourself that is admirable, and you have the added advantage—in talking about your quirks—of coming off as humorous, likable, or just plain human. The other advantage of quirky topics is that they FORCE you to describe things: the Costco essay, for instance, is rich with colors, physical comedy, and brand names. Choosing such a topic makes it that much harder for you to fall short on details and specifics.

But not all quirks are created equal. To see why—and to see how to get the RIGHT quirks into your personal statement—take a spin through the Quirk Questionnaire provided on the following page.

Done? Once you have your quirks figured out, ask yourself the standard question below.

• ***Which quirks bring out my most remarkable personal traits?***

For Brittany Stinson, that trait was inquisitiveness. For Carolina Williams, that trait was self-sufficiency. And for you, that trait could be any meaningful quality that was presented on Pages 14-

The Quirk Questionnaire

- According to your FRIENDS, what is the weirdest thing about you?

  _____

- According to your FAMILY, what is the weirdest thing about you?

  _____

- What hobbies, interests, collections, or obsessions do you have that you mentioned NOWHERE in Chapter 1?

  _____

  _____

  ....

- If you could spend a day doing ANYTHING, what would you do?

  _____

  _____

- What is the strangest thing you have ever done?

  _____

  _____

Name your favorite . . .

Food: _____   TV Show/Film: _____

Band: _____   Way to Relax: _____

15 (Questionnaire) or Pages 28-31 (Pros and Cons). Sometimes, it takes a quirk to express that trait in all its power and complexity.

Part 2: Breaking the Format

Here's another question. On the face of it, which of these ways of structuring an essay is superior?

1. Explaining an challenge that you faced as an athlete, outlining how you made efforts to overcome the challenge, pointing out positive outcomes

2. Comparing your dream college to a pita

Again, consider how these topics would work in theory and in practice. As with essays that are quirk-based, the results here are illuminating—though, at least at first glance, rather odd.

In Theory

If you picked Topic 1, you probably assumed that the writer had developed a clear structure for a discussion of a significant activity and an admirable set of qualities. What the writer hopes to communicate about determination and hard work is by no means in doubt—nor is the fact that the essay will have some narrative movement. Unless all goes wrong, there will be a discernible beginning, middle, and end to this essay.

As for Topic 2 . . . seriously, a pita? Isn't that risky, corny, or downright weird?

It turns out, though, that pita sandwiches are wonderful in many ways: hearty flavors, reasonable nutritional value, AND top-level college acceptances. Though risky, talking about a pita—and doing so for a major structuring principle, no less—works better here.

In Practice

Well, if you picked Topic 1, you clearly didn't read Chapter 1 of this book closely enough. An essay oriented around athletics can be effective, but the essay outlined on the previous page is based on a dangerously clichéd "overcoming challenges" structure that is criticized on Page 23. The likelihood that writer's sheer craft can rise above a base structure this trite is dismally low.

As for Topic 2, this one was in fact used by a student who earned a Class of 2020 acceptance to Johns Hopkins. (Read more at https://apply.jhu.edu/essays-that-worked-2020/.) The essay itself, titled "The Palate of My Mind," was praised by the admissions committee for one "exciting" trait in particular: where the applicant was concerned, the essay revealed "something about her that we couldn't learn through any other part of her application—her favorite food." This is EXACTLY what even a traditional essay should do—reveal a new insight, even when the topic is a long-term, well-appreciated extracurricular, not a "hummus-tabouli wrap."

The Unconventional Structures

If you are going to use an unconventional structure, you will need to ask yourself two key questions about your chosen format.

1. *Is my chosen structure imaginative and engaging, or just desperate and corny?*

2. *Does my chosen structure still provide a sense of logic and coherence in terms of messaging?*

Any essay that assumes an unconventional structure must pass these tests. Fortunately, there are a few offbeat formats and premises that students have used, with reliable enough results even in drafting stages, to be worth citing immediately.

Extended Analogy

While this format already has a respectable track record thanks to that Hopkins-as-a-hummus-tabouli-wrap essay, the possibilities don't end there. Not by a long shot. Any clever, appropriate comparison between one of your experiences and a rather unexpected, ultimately illuminating piece of the world is fair game here.

For instance, imagine that you are in a business-oriented club or extracurricular. Have any of your experiences reminded you of being a contestant on *Shark Tank* or a character on *Succession*? Try the analogy out as a means of structuring the essay, if so. Or, imagine that you enjoy exploring museums on the weekend. What does the experience feel like? A treasure hunt? An old-school video game? A day inside a surrealist painting?

These are some possibilities. Whatever you do, though, DON'T FORCE an analogy in the belief that having a relatively strange format of this sort will automatically elevate the essay. You need an analogy that helps the reader to see your creative side, and readers can be surprisingly good at calling out failed attempts at originality.

Ingenious Document (With Caution)

Can you format your essay as a guidebook article, a short script, or a short story? It is forbiddingly difficult to do so, but it is possible. The purpose of using such an "ingenious" document format is to deliver information in a clever and attention-getting way. Just make sure that the information ITSELF is insightful and interesting, and use second opinions aggressively here to make sure that the essay would not be superior if organized traditionally.

CAUTION: Do not write a poem, or a letter to yourself.

Why? First, poetry. Unless you are a practiced creative writer, a good poem is probably hard to pull off under any circumstances. A bad poem is more likely to seem like a cringeworthy nursery rhyme or a terrible first draft of a meditation exercise than like anything else.

Second, the letter to yourself. This format probably allows you to deliver some clear themes and ideas, but runs into dangers of its own. It is a notoriously silly and self-indulgent format. Moreover, as you will see in the chapter on supplementals (Pages 93-95 especially), using a letter-like format ANYWHERE on a college application is tough to do effectively.

Extended Reflection (With Caution)

Perhaps you have several thoughts, memories, and imaginings that are fascinating but a bit difficult to pull together in a gradually-explained standard form. You can, at the very least, TRY to commit some of your free-flowing ideas to paper. This isn't quite a full "stream of consciousness" essay format, but you do have more liberty to deliver ideas spontaneously. Also, us italics for your more whimsical sections to set them off as, well, moments of whimsy.

CAUTION: Do not make your whole essay reflective or whimsical in this way.

Why? You need some passages that will orient the reader and put what it all means in perspective. Again, a good essay of this sort will read like a good standard essay, just a bit more spontaneous than usual. That means that paragraphs of clear-headed reflection should stand out from your musings.

Also, do NOT devote this essay to minor observations that don't lead to anything more. Nobody cares what the woodgrain of your bedroom floor looks like, on its own. But if you an accomplished violinist who is attentive the construction of instruments, or a devoted collage artist with an interest in woodgrain textures, then woodgrain starts to matter.

Part 5

The Supplemental Essays

Beyond the Main Essay
The Most Important Strategies

Supplemental Essay Ground Rules

Depending on the applications that you have chosen to file, you may be nearly at the end of your time devising college essays—or may only be at the beginning. The latter case is most common if you are facing an application with a substantial required second essay (as has historically been the case with UPenn) or a series of short responses instead of a core personal statement (as has historically been the case with MIT). In any case, you should know SOMETHING about what a good supplemental looks like in case your college wish list shifts a bit.

Regardless of specifics, there is one core requirement that a good personal statement and a good supplemental essay will share.

- *Unless directed otherwise, you must ALWAYS have SOME NARRATIVE elements in a supplemental essay.*

Lists of preferences (one type of supplemental) present an exception to this premise. Otherwise, the goal of a supplemental is not to deliver a research paper or an Ivy League advertisement; the point is to draw the reader in and describe your life at its most intriguing.

83

Your Academic Choices

One of the most common types of supplemental essay will ask you to explain your academic plans. These will normally NOT be as long as Common App essays, but they will demand similar standards of writing prowess and attention to detail. They will also require you to deal with questions that are much less open-ended.

• **Why do you want to go to this particular SCHOOL?**

• **Why do you want to study this particular MAJOR?**

The phrasing may vary, but the issues at hand, essentially, are the two above. Fortunately, you can use a very straightforward format for excellent results here, and that format is largely a shortened version of the format for the Common App personal statement.

Format for School or Major Questions

Think of these as Common App essays with only two stages, one specific, one general.

1. **Start with a short narrative or descriptive portion that leads into a discussion of the relevant school or major.**

2. **Finish with an explanation of how your passions and interests align, in specific terms, with the school or major.**

The principles of the expected writing style also hold constant. You want to share your experience and knowledge in a manner that is clear, precise, insightful, and yet lively and spontaneous. And you want to make sure that these supplemental essays are interesting and personable as stand-alone pieces of writing.

These guidelines can't be stressed enough. Some students wrongly assume that supplements require a degree of formality and technicality that the main personal statement doesn't. Such an approach, sadly, results in essays that read like the disclaimers on over-the-counter medicines. As the next few pages show, an approach of this sort can also poison an otherwise good application with a tone that is at once self-important and strangely uninformed.

Sheer boredom is not the only problem with such an approach, either. The bigger liability is that a seemingly "professional" but actually dry, overly-technical essay does nothing to communicate PASSION for your chosen major and school. Showing in vital, emotional terms why you want to devote four years of your life to a school—and the rest of your life, perhaps, to a field of study—needs to be one of your priorities.

So, you know the basics, and you know what you need to achieve. Consider the School and Major supplements individually, and see how to make each type stand out on its own terms.

"Why This College?" Supplement

Aside from presenting a miniature narrative, supplemental essays that address your college choice must explain your rationale for wanting to attend. That rationale must itself be intriguing. In the interest of knowing your enemies, here are some uninteresting reasons for wanting to attend a specific school.

AVOID Uninteresting Reasoning

1. **Variety of majors and classes**

2. **Students are high-achieving, like I am**

3. **School is prestigious or world-renowned**

4. **School is famous for [Insert Over-Used Factoid Right Here]**

Why are these reasons so bad? The first two (the curriculum, and the student body) are painfully obvious facts about ANY highly-ranked university. Devoting an essay to either of these lines of thought would be a massive failure of creativity.

The third and fourth are even worse, perhaps, but in different ways. Bad reason number three is indeed obvious (OF COURSE Brown or Northwestern or UCLA is "prestigious") but has another drawback: do you really want to present yourself to admissions readers as the kind of person who obsesses over school rankings? Does anyone? Simply or even MOSTLY wanting to go to a school because it is "world-renowned" is a sign of poor character: snobbishness, reductive thinking, you name it.

Bad reason number four is harder to gauge, so develop your instincts. Pointing out that NYU is in New York, or that Notre Dame has a famous football team, is the kind of groan-inducer that fits the bill.

"Why This Major?" Supplement

For supplementary essays that are slanted towards your choice of major, you may feel on somewhat surer footing at first. A few of the traps for this type of essay, after all, are pretty obvious. Consider for instance the kind of reasoning you should avoid at all costs.

AVOID Damaging Reasoning

1. **I've always done it.**

2. **I have a lot of activities in it.**

3. **I get the best grades in it.**

4. **My brother or sister was in it.**

5. **My parents want me to.**

6. **I'll make good money.**

These reasons are listed from least to most awful. (Unless, of course, you are trying to lift yourself out of poverty. And if you are, why didn't you say so on the Common App?) In the vast majority of cases, these "rationales"—if you can somehow dignify them with that term—show little or no independent thinking. They may show enthusiasm, but of the worst kind: a sort of grasping, striving enthusiasm that is fun enough on TV melodramas but radioactive on a college essay.

Instead of courting any of these theme- or topic-based problems, try out the Supplemental Essay Questionnaire on the page that follows. As you did with the Personal Statement questionnaire, you will figure out how to present your personal strengths. You will ALSO figure out, this time, how to create an essay that balances your life with information about your college or major that is as far from cliché as humanly possible.

Style and Structure

After you have determined what to write about for the college- and major-oriented supplements, you will need to watch out for a few recurring editing problems. Some of these, in fact, can arise more often here than they do in the Personal Statement.

The Supplemental Essay Questionnaire

- List three IMPORTANT and LESSER-KNOWN facts about the college that you are discussing.

1. _____

2. _____

3. _____

- Why do you want to go to this college (one phrase or sentence)?

_____

_____

- Why is your personality a good fit for your desired college (one phrase or sentence)?

_____

_____

- List three INTERESTING EVENTS from your life. Each one must be related to your major.

1. _____

2. _____

3. _____

- Why are you gravitating to this major, and why is it a good fit for your personality (one phrase or sentence)?

_____

_____

Style: DO Be Aggressive About Sentence Variety

When you are ready to revise the essay, go back to Chapter 3 and make sure that you take all of the advice in that portion of the book to heart. There is, in fact, a signature danger that you need to avoid for college and major supplementals. Too many of these essays start off as barrages of "I want to . . . " and "I am fascinated by . . . " statements, and you must move beyond such an awkward start to establish a much more elegant progression of ideas.

Of course, checklists always help. You can use the spare copies of the Proofreading and Second Opinion Checklists on Pages 122-125 to make sure that your essay has reasonable variety in terms of sentence openings, sentence structures, and sentence lengths.

Style: DON'T Let Clichés Slip In

Once you are done with the essay, give it a second run to make sure that NONE of the banalities under the "AVOID" lists (Pages 86 -87) slipped in. It is possible that they will sneak through simply if you let your guard down, or if you are trying to express passion but can't find the right words. Spend time replacing any vague, deficient ideas with thoughts that are crisp and original.

Structure: DO Consider a "Circular" Organization

You have already been advised to start any given supplemental with a miniature narrative, and even a 100-word supplemental should give you space (say, 25-40 words) for one strong scene. If you are writing a much more detailed supplemental, try to return to that opening narrative by reiterating a detail, memory, or moment from it at the end. Doing so will give the essay a clear shape. And this firm structuring is an asset that should not be underestimated here, because too many supplementals can start reading like laundry lists of random facts about majors, departments, and universities.

These stylistic rules will not vary especially much—or at all—for the other supplemental essays that you may encounter. Keep in mind that you need some specialized information and a striking narrative for ANY supplemental and you will be fine, even when the topics (as you will see below) are difficult or perplexing at first.

"Favorite Activity" Supplement

Well, come to think of it, this one shouldn't be difficult or perplexing at all. The logical first step would be to return to the Profile-at-a-Glance Questionnaire on Pages 14-15; you can also run the Questionnaire again using the extra copies on Pages 118-121.

From there, you will mostly write an essay that 1) begins with a narrative and 2) concludes with a broader discussion. You can address the significance of your chosen activity, your future with it, or your one or two most fulfilling memories in the second stage. Stay specific, but make an argument for why your activity matters.

There is one other piece of advice for dealing with the "favorite activity" supplement. If you can successfully avoid both bragging and simply bombarding your reader with bland facts, you will need to exercise care in one other way.

- *Be CAUTIOUS of writing about the SAME ACTIVITY in two major portions of an application.*

You don't want the admissions readers to think that your life is completely one-note—EVEN if the activity is important or complex, EVEN if returning to the same topic seems to unify your application. However, there is a (tricky) middle ground.

- *If you DO RETURN to a topic, approach a DIFFERENT ELEMENT and a DIFFERENT THEME from your life.*

Can you ever treat a supplemental as a throwaway?

Short answer: normally, you shouldn't. When the stakes are high, an essay that reads like a lazy copy and paste will do you no favors.

Okay. Then what about the guy who simply wrote #BlackLivesMatter 100 times and got into Stanford?

In 2017, a student named Ziad Ahmed responded to a Stanford University application question ("What matters to you, and why?") by writing "#BlackLivesMatter" one hundred times. (Read more about Ahmed at https://www.cnn.com/2017/04/05/us/stanford-application-black-lives-matter-trnd/index.html.) He got in, but his essay does NOT offer a template for supplementals in any way. There are a few good explanations for what happened with Ahmed's Stanford acceptance.

1. Ahmed was already an outstanding student (one who also got into Princeton and Yale, no less) and decided to take a gamble that admissions readers would look past.

2. Ahmed's answer was but one essay on a multi-essay application (which it was, as a 100- to 250-word short answer on an application that also required a fully-developed personal statement).

Here, the gamble worked. Yet it was one gamble, and it was too clever and risky to be easily imitated.

Consider the following possibility: you are actively involved in the Youth Group for your church, take the most pride in your accomplishments with this organization, and want to be a very active member of a campus ministry in college. You could—and in some cases probably should—make this the topic of your main essay. If you have a supplemental, though, and this *is* your favorite activity, use an element of your experience that you did NOT address in the personal statement—a different year, a different service project, a different retreat. After all, your years in college will call for focus, and readers may be impressed to see that you can have multiple perspectives on a single strong commitment.

"Social Issue" Supplement

This essay is among the more widely misinterpreted supplements. Honors colleges and international studies programs often ask students to weigh in on debates—political, social, economic, cultural—that are of global importance. Even though you must provide analysis, you must NOT forget to bring in a narrative element.

As you brainstorm this one, focus on the following reminder (from Page 83) until it gets stuck in your head like a bad pop song.

- *. . . you must ALWAYS have NARRATIVE elements . . .*

The central problem with the social issue supplement is that writers often approach these as though they are expository articles or term papers. Most of the writing that results is 1) boring and 2) unhelpful. College admissions committees want to hear about YOU, not get a summary of developments in journalistic ethics or foreign affairs.

So, force yourself to start with a narrative and move into a more analytic portion. And reflect on issues that REALLY INTEREST you before writing. If you have some flexibility in choice of topic (the generic "an issue that is important to you"), read through a comprehensive newspaper like *The New York Times* or *The Wall Street Journal* and see what attracts your interest. And if you have less flexibility (the issue or the field more clearly chosen for you), do a LOT of brainstorming on your personal angle before you do any research.

Also, know your clichés. Don't use an invitation to write on virtually any issue to inadvertently go with an issue that is overbearingly common. As of this writing (spring of 2020), it is unclear whether the COVID-19 crisis will be over-discussed on social issue essays. It's possible that it will, so be cautious if you say anything about it and make sure that you have a UNIQUE and PERSONAL approach.

One thing is certain, though: unless you have a large number of political extracurriculars, a discussion of anything Donald Trump-related will be among the worst clichés you can find. Is there a more obvious news item? A more exhausting one? Just avoid, and find something that has not been publicized to death over the past four years.

"Letter to a Roommate" Stanford University

It is a good idea, right off the bat, to say a word or two about the signature danger of this supplement.

- *This essay can give a somewhat unfiltered view of your personality. It should NOT be borderline incoherent.*

The "letter to a roommate" supplement that Stanford has long utilized tempts writer after writer to fit in as many quirky and endearing traits as possible. Such an impulse is natural. After all, if you are going to be rooming with someone for a whole year, you want to be as clear as possible about your goals, ambitions, habits, and passions, right? That's how a letter like this might help your future roommate. But a loose collection of tics and anecdotes probably won't amount to a clear message to the admissions committee—your REAL readers here.

One of the best things you can do with this essay is return to the Quirk Questionnaire on Page 76. (Additional copies are available on Pages 126-127.) From there, find a trait and a message that are CLEARLY central to who you are, then work to bring in other things that are interesting about you without losing sight of your key theme and topic.

Imagine, for instance, that you are writing five paragraphs about yourself. Here is what the outline of a rather pointless "letter to a roommate" supplement will look like.

P1: Giant collection of model planes; also built model rockets **X**

P2: Went to Greenland last winter as part of Christmas trip **X**

P3: Volunteered at an animal shelter despite a cat allergy **X**

P4: Took an elective course on social psychology **X**

P5: Looking for a restaurant that makes a perfect cheesesteak **X**

Now, lively and personable writing could salvage this structure. But why not write an essay that makes you look like something other than a Buzzfeed article? On the next page, you will find a version that has some interesting little side notes and a strong undertone based on a single set of interests in flight and aerospace. Notice that the writer isn't PERFECTLY on topic all the time. Still, there is enough of a motive the entire piece of writing that the digressions can delight the reader—not destabilize the entire essay.

94

P1: Giant collection of model planes; bringing a few to college ✔

P2: Flew to Greenland on a single-engine plane last Christmas ✔

P3: Obsessed with *Top Gun*; best friends all have code names ✔

P4: Volunteering and 4H, memories of building model rockets ✔

P5: Cheesesteak, cat allergy, quick finish with aerospace topic ✔

"Lists of Favorites"
Columbia University

Historically, Columbia University has asked students to list favorite "books you read for pleasure," "publications and websites," and "entertainments." There are two ground rules to these supplementals.

1. *FOLLOW THE FORMAT: just list the items, AVOID NARRATIVE for once, and use explanations (date, medium, brief description) primarily when needed for clarity*

2. *BE HONEST <u>AND</u> INTERESTING: never be misleading or deceptive about your preferences, but reflect to figure out great choices that may not be so obvious at first*

The first rule is rather self-explanatory. With these supplementals, well-informed readers can use your lists to piece together more about your personality. For your part, use the lists to highlight your dedication to activities and subjects raised elsewhere on your application—or to demonstrate your versatility.

This is where the second rule comes in. You can't lie about what you've read or done, but if you're a strong candidate for admission to any elite college or university, you shouldn't need to anyway. Nonetheless, you should accept that the best items for one of these lists will probably not be the first ones you think of.

Consider the books that you have read. Off the top of your head, which ones would you list as the ones you enjoyed the most? Here are a few titles that may be familiar.

- *Hamlet*; *Romeo and Juliet*; *The Scarlet Letter*; *The Great Gatsby*; *The Catcher in the Rye*; *The Lord of the Flies*; *To Kill a Mockingbird* (ALL WIDELY EXPECTED CHOICES)

If you are thinking of using any one of these, take heed. All of the books named above are EXTREMELY common on high school reading lists and are fair game for Columbia's frequent question about "required readings." It's fine if you honestly enjoyed *The Great Gatsby* and want to say so. In contrast, it is absolutely NOT fine if you have read so little that ALL your lists of preferences amount to one giant copy-and-paste of a World Literature syllabus.

Think of it this way: if you did enjoy *The Great Gatsby*, why didn't you seek out other works by F. Scott Fitzgerald? Start reflecting. Any book or other source that is truly going to make it onto a list of favorites probably led you to make new connections and seek out further knowledge. So yes, *The Great Gatsby* on its own looks a bit suspicious. However, *The Great Gatsby* along with *This Side of Paradise*, *The Last Tycoon*, or "Babylon Revisited" will show that your experience with Fitzgerald's fiction really mattered.

While making the lists, keep in mind two additional pieces of advice.

1. **Delve into Your Major and Activities:** Even though you SHOULDN'T give the impression that everything you do is major-related—because, for the sake of your sanity, it probably isn't—you should think hard to bring up major-related items. Are you a dedicated athlete? Well, then pointing out that you

read *Shoe Dog* and *The Mamba Mentality*—provided that you actually did—is all to your advantage. Are you an aspiring business major? Then don't be shy about how much time you spend reading MarketWatch and watching CNBC.

2. **Don't Be Too Afraid of Pop Culture:** When discussed honestly and tactfully, pop culture references can reveal a lot about who you are. Keep in mind that pop culture topics—from anime to hip hop to fan fiction—often come in for analysis by award-winning journalists and tenured university professors. Use pop culture sparingly but wisely, stay away from the stuff that is mostly junk or empty provocation (Looking at you, reality TV.), and use a second reader to make sure that your pop culture references convey the message and image that you want.

"Weird, Random Topics" University of Chicago

Here are some of the past topics that the University of Chicago has floated for its applicants.

- "Cats have nine lives, Pac-Man has 3 lives, and radioactive isotopes have half-lives. How many lives does something else—conceptual or actual—have, and why?"

- "Joan of Arkansas. Queen Elizabeth Cady Stanton. Babe Ruth Bader Ginsburg. Mash up a historical figure with a new time period, environment, location, or occupation, and tell us their story."

- "How are apples and oranges supposed to be compared? Possible answers involve, but are not limited to, statistics, chemistry, physics, linguistics, and philosophy."

Essays such as these are meant to highlight the applicant's creativity. There are very few constraints with the UChicago supplement—

and applicants can sometimes resort to prompts from earlier years (as explained at https://collegeadmissions.uchicago.edu/apply/uchicago-supplemental-essay-questions) or create their own prompts.

So how do you deal with either an unusual degree of liberty or a prompt that narrows itself down in a strange manner—or both at once? Here are a few guidelines.

1. Revisit the "Breaking the Rules" chapter of this book for guidance in terms of managing a strange yet meaningful essay.

2. Do a lot of process of elimination as you look through the prompts, and see if you can find two or three that are truly intriguing.

3. See if you can "reverse-engineer" the themes and message of one of your more traditional essays to fit a non-traditional prompt.

4. Don't assume that a quirky format is enough to win over readers, since small details, vivid descriptions, and real emotion will always matter.

Once you have a decent first draft of this essay, find a good second reader and focus on the following question.

- ***Is my approach both 1) genuinely original and 2) truly meaningful in what it communicates about my character?***

Strange format or no strange format, the UChicago supplement functions much like any college essay. It communicates who you are, and in doing so provides a high-stakes, high-reward opportunity to take creative liberties that can say a lot about your personality.

Complete Sample Personal Statements

Transforming Your Essay
Two Samples, Before and After

Ground Rules

If there is one thing that this book emphasizes in its early stages, it's that few application essays are automatically hopeless. (The complete list of sure-fire duds is available on Pages 8-11.) For most essays, a writer may be struggling to avoid a cliché approach to a promising topic. Or may be tripped up by a style that fails to impress. Or may have a few powerful images that fail to amount to a meaningful, coherent message.

This section gives you four essays—two originals with some decent fundamentals and unbearably poor execution, and two re-writes that exhibit mastery of the lessons in this book. Read these to see 1) if anything you have written bears a troubling resemblance content from the awful essays and 2) if any of your writing is as impressive as the work present in the awesome ones.

Above all, don't be intimidated. Moving an essay from awful to awesome is sometimes an intensive process. Here, you will only see the beginning and end results, but should nonetheless discern the lines of reasoning that can transform any essay on a solid-enough topic into a masterpiece of a personal statement.

101

Sample 1: Grace S.
X Where the Essay Began X

One of the elements that has distinguished me throughout my time in high school has been my abiding devotion to the world of fine art. From my childhood onward, I was intrigued by the masterpieces of painting and sculpture that the finest minds in art history have produced; moreover, I have used my high school curriculum, namely my coursework in AP Art History and AP World History, to pursue this long-term interest in an academic setting. Indeed, a career in art history is a valid possibility, and my current interests in this respect include working directly with a museum to help others to understand important works of art.

I am also, nonetheless, defined by my participation in activities that complement this interest. My school its notable for its robust number of extracurricular clubs, and of these I have been especially drawn to those that revolve around sociopolitical debate and activism. Since freshman year, I have been an active and engaged member of the student council, serving first as Treasurer for my own class, then as Secretary for Student Life (a job that immersed me in the planning of entertainment and recreation events that drew together the school community in an engaging manner). Most recently, I was instrumental in using graphic design software to create banners and brochures for our school's Pride Day, a celebration of LGBTQ+ lifestyle choices and public acceptance. Furthermore, I have used this background to create materials for less prominent events, including weekly "coffeehouse" chat and poetry reading sessions in our student lounge.

Last year, I built on these leadership activities by attending the Future Financial Leaders of America conference at the University of North Carolina, Chapel Hill. Over the course of ten days, I collaborated with other young people who hailed from diverse communities all over the United States, and sometimes well beyond. Together, we designed innovative projects that addressed various issues in sustainable urban development, cultural anthropology, and economics for developing markets. The program culminated in a research symposium that displayed our work to a panel that brought together UNC faculty members, and that required us to translate our ideas into accessible PowerPoint form.

I have also complemented my role in pre-professional development seminars by remaining active in the athletics, both varsity and recreational, offered at the boarding school that I attend. I am currently a member of the Tennis Team, and have refined my skills over the years to the point that I am now playing both second and first doubles, depending on the composition of the team and the placement of a given match in the season schedule. In less competitive settings, I have been active in the informal Ping Pong Club, and regularly make use of our school's athletic facilities to play basketball, softball, and soccer with my peers.

In looking towards my future career prospects, I am drawn to professions that value a combination of critical thinking and creativity. I have already begun to explore my options by immersing myself in professional environments; this past summer, I served an unpaid internship at the American Visionary Art Museum in Baltimore. This experience was instrumental in refining my interpersonal and time-management skills. I also continue to explore my prospects by participating in the various career-oriented evening lectures that my school hosts. It is my belief that college will help me to attain the guidance necessary to use my many talents in the pursuit of both social change and personal growth.

Why this essay FAILS

There is not a single significant error in grammar or vocabulary in this essay: in fact, its considerable variety in sentence structure indicates that it has been expertly proofread. But there is NOT a single memorable description, scene, or moment of dialogue, either. As a narrative that would engage an admissions reader, this essay fails in almost every respect imaginable.

What the original essay reads like, instead, is a resume translated into prose. The redundancy involved in this situation is bad enough, though what makes the whole situation worse is the fact that the essay does not in any way have a sense of priority. No one activity ever becomes a meaningful focus. No theme can ever emerge to unify the essay and to suggest something noteworthy about Grace's values or personality.

Fortunately, there IS a point of possible development that a careful reader might detect. Grace both began and finished off with references to her art historical interests. This is a topic that could be rich with descriptive potential but that should NOT be talked about in a predominantly academic manner, as Grace discussed artistic matters early on. Instead, the more interesting topic could be Grace's internship at the American Visionary Art Museum. Here is the essay, transformed into a truly engaging narrative.

Sample 1: Grace S.
✔ The Final Essay ✔

A whirligig that stands 24 feet tall; trees spangled with mirrors, Christmas lights, and costume jewelry; neon plastic sculptures of Buddha and Satan and Marilyn Monroe. There is a whole world—no, an entire universe—of oddity to notice at the American Visionary Art Museum, where offbeat and maximalistic folk art finds a home. Yet you probably won't notice me. More likely, you'll walk up to the coatcheck, drop off your bags or stroller for me to put in a safe place, take the ticket I hand you, and walk right past.

And that is as it should be. After all, how am I—the humble unpaid intern working the coat check—supposed to upstage a throne covered entirely with bottle caps or a model ocean liner made entirely out of toothpicks? (Yes, the AVAM has those too.) You have five floors of unleashed nuttiness to explore, and I have my duties. Raincoats and umbrellas. And something else, something that is its own privilege and challenge.

Invisibility.

If there was one thing I had to learn most of all, in my first weeks of interning, it was how to deal with being un-seen, un-heard. It was a tough lesson for an only child—and for an outspoken student from a 400-student prep school in Delaware. I was accustomed to being listened to or at least to being heard, to debating politics with my friends and the virtues of Abstract Expressionism with my mad genius of an art history teacher. For once, as an intern, I was in the background.

Yet invisibility has its perks, some obvious, some hard earned. Invisibility was a condition I had so often discussed, examined, analyzed, but never really known for myself as intensely as I did then. I had spent my high school years standing up for fast food workers every time the question "Should we raise the minimum wage?" was thrown my way. Now I knew what it was like to spend hours repeating the same task. I had stood up for the Van Goghs and Dickinsons of the world every time the idea of "unappreciated brilliance" arose. Now I knew what it was like to have a mind churning with new stories, and a legion of sketch pads and canvases at home, and to wonder if any of what I had created would find its proper audience.

And I learned that invisibility, though often a burden, is sometimes a gift.

In the moments between sorting through coats and bags, I would train my mind not on a book or an iPad (both off-limits during work hours) but on anything and everything. My thoughts would roam to the characters in my latest story, who were still sitting in a cafe in Munich or a bus station in Siberia, waiting for their moment of crisis to arrive. Other times, my mind would stray to the old woman I had begun to sketch: her head was all finished, but she was still desperately in need of legs and arms (and probably not too happy about it). Always, though, my ideas would amble back the museum itself, to its collection of magnificent oddities. Before locking up, I would make sure to personally follow my thoughts right there, to see the galaxy of shadow puppets and collages and carvings that drew me to the Visionary Art Museum when I was only a grammar schooler and that will keep drawing me back even when my coat checking days are well behind me.

So when you visit, just drop off your things, take your ticket, and stride right past. A kind word might be appreciated, but it isn't necessary, because you're walking into a museum that has given me so much—art, perspective, invisibility—and that I hope gives you something equally powerful. I'm the girl at the coat check. And I contain multitudes.

Sample 2: Lawrence Z.
X Where the Essay Began X

According to esteemed football player and NFL coach Vince Lombardi, "The price of success is hard work, dedication to the job at hand, and the determination that whether we win or lose, we have applied the best of ourselves to the task at hand." In life, we all face a multitude of tasks that push us to achieve our best results, and many of those results may be construed as the result of determination to achieve specific and worthwhile goals. For me, the moment of challenge arose during the championship meet of my high school's varsity swim team, of which I also serve as treasurer and publicist for a local newspaper.

As a sophomore, I had worked with great determination to improve my times in the events that I normally swam during swim meets. By practicing consistently and by asking for advice, I had found ways to enhance my performance as an athlete, but I realized that I would need to do more to rise to the occasion when the final swim meet of the year arrived. Eager for help that would enable me to target specific skills, I consulted with other members of the team, and we arrived at a workout schedule that I would implement along with my usual practices. At first, I realized that the plan that we had arrived at cooperatively might nonetheless be intimidating to some athletes. However, I knew that improving my time and contributing to the team would require me to do more than I had ever done before in order to contribute to our success.

When the meet itself drew extremely close, I expended as much effort as I could to make sure that I did not let my fellow team members down. In fact, I privately made a few alterations to the advice that the older team members had given me, though I knew that these alterations would enable me to meet my goals in a manner that was more suitable to my unique set of skills and abilities. Then, on the day of the meet, I made sure that I was rested, and that I was mentally prepared to put forward an effort that would reward the good faith of the older team members who had dedicated their time to analyzing my performance. Ultimately, the time that I achieved was more than five seconds faster than my previous best time in any event.

It is commonly argued that some goals may seem so difficult to achieve that forsaking the effort would be a wiser choice than continuing with an effort that appears to offer a small chance of success. However, as Og Mandino once noted, "Failure will never overtake me if my determination to succeed is strong enough." Advice such as this has indeed inspired me considerably, as I have used my work throughout high school to display efforts of determination and will power that will inspire the broader community that witnesses my positive qualities. Together, for instance, my varsity swim team and I have both performed exceptionally well in our formal meets and engaged in charitable efforts that show that we are committed athletes who have the power to offer others reassurance and motivation. Moreover, in the variety of extracurricular activities that I have pursued, I have attained the positive interpersonal characteristics that are destined to make me an asset to a variety of academic and professional settings. By taking these qualities together, I intend to have a lasting impact on the various individuals whom I encounter and who will benefit from my spirit of proactivity and determination.

Why this essay FAILS

Unlike Grace's initial essay, Lawrence's first attempt at a personal statement exhibited something of a narrative structure. Unfortunately, this narrative structure was filled out with details that were hazy at best. At worst, Lawrence's writing lapsed into extremely vague language that primarily served the purpose of boasting about his positive qualities. If this essay reaches an especially weary reader, the rather condescending tone may be enough to send Lawrence's application straight to the rejection pile.

Fortunately, although the tone of this essay is regrettable, the topic can be salvaged. Lawrence's writing includes references to the other swimmers on the team. While preserving the over-used "try hard and win in athletics" structure of the essay would be a mistake, arriving at a new theme for this athletics topic is a possibility. Discussing mentorship, cooperation, or friendship (or some combination of these qualities) among athletes at different skill levels would give this essay a much more original overall approach.

Some of Lawrence's writing choices, of course, should be automatically rejected. Beginning with a quotation, instead of beginning with a hook that clearly relates to the writer's own life, is a complete distraction under most circumstances. With radical revisions, Lawrence was able to craft an essay that combines vivid descriptions with analysis that is concrete, thoughtful, and rich in the kind of personality that an admissions reader would find appealing.

Sample 2: Lawrence Z.
✔ The Final Essay ✔

It's 5:30 in the morning on a Saturday, and all fourteen of us should be in bed. Instead, we're sitting in abandoned chemistry classroom, chowing down on bagels and watching clips from *Braveheart* and *Saving Private Ryan*—our way of getting motivated for the swim meet ahead. Then it's a two-and-a-half-hour ride in a school bus that looks like it's been around since 1972, and then a full day of racing so hard we feel like our lungs are turning to lava. For now, though, it's us, some World War II movies, and the calm before the storm.

"This never gets old," says O'Neil, the team captain, who's heading to the University of Miami on a swimming scholarship next year. Soldiers are storming across the screen. He takes a huge bite of his bagel and declares, "Mum-mum-mufflump!"

"What?" says Carlo, the second-fastest backstroker on the team.

"I said," says O'Neil, now finished chewing, "they're just like us."

"Yeah," I say as an explosion erupts onscreen, sending a soldier flying right across the battlefield and landing him in a ditch. "And that guy you just saw is me."

The whole room bursts out laughing.

It's no secret that I'm not the world's greatest swimmer: if you were a five-five with a minor heart condition, would you be trying to be the next Michael Phelps? I sure hope not, but I never had my sights on the Olympics anyway when I joined my school's varsity—and for the record only—swim team. My goal was different:

111

to get exercise and make some new friends. Maybe, I thought, I would also emerge as a leader, despite not having much of an idea how to do butterfly when I signed up.

However, I soon discovered that "leader" was the wrong word for anyone on the team. There were swimmers who stood above the rest, but they did not make any of us feel inferior in any way. Rather, they pushed me and the other guys with middling times to be better, to work more, to realize that we might have the ability to rise in the ranks with the right amount of practice. What would happen if we didn't? Even then, we would still be one of the team, one of the guys you could call if you needed help studying for AP Econ or just wanted to talk about life for a couple hours. In the water we were about competition, but everywhere else we were our own band of brothers.

*　*　*

I've just finished my fourth and last race of the meet. I lunge out of the water, wobble over to the team, and sit down like I never want to get up again. O'Neil ambles over.

"Lawrence, did you see what you just did out there?"

"No," I say. Right now I feel like an earthquake has hit every joint in my body.

"You shaved like five seconds off your best time, that's what you did."

"Are we going to Wendy's after this?" I ask, barely capable of putting words together.

"Hell yeah we're going to Wendy's!"

We may wonder if close connection is possible today; technology, the argument goes, has been more successful in driving people apart than in bringing them together. Fair enough. But then there is the antidote, the determination to connect that being part of a team has instilled in me. Whether my future takes me to a lab or a law firm or an investment bank, I know that my role is to be a part of something bigger, something that succeeds or fails based on its ability to come together, not its determination to promote a few and leave the rest behind. There's an old saying that "if you want to go fast, go alone; if you want to go far, go together." I am determined to go far, whatever form that takes, and swimming has taught me how potent and how enjoyable it is not to go alone.

NOTE

Additional Essay Samples

Helpful Resources

With the proliferation of college forums and college prep sites, sample essays aren't especially hard to find if you have a good Internet connection. Yet finding the RIGHT essays is a somewhat trickier task. After all, if the Internet can deliver fake news, the Internet can also deliver fake college essay success stories.

To cut through the unreliability, try starting with the following two sites.

- GradeSaver.com offers a database of college essays—which are separated out by school and designated by question prompt—for interested college students. There were are 2500 samples here as of the last count (spring 2020). Many of the recently-posted essays meet the standards of excellence outlined in this book. Some, amazingly, exceed those standards. Also, full disclosure, one of our own editors manages this portion of the site.

- Johns Hopkins University regularly publishes an "Essays that Worked" feature on its institutional web site: the most recent version can be found at *https://apply.jhu.edu/application-process/essays-that-worked/*. Regardless of topic and theme, the Hopkins samples will give you excellent specimens of hooks, sensory descriptions, and other narrative elements that a winning college essay demands.

Additional Questionnaires

The Profile-at-a-Glance
QUESTIONNAIRE

DIRECTIONS: Respond to the questions quickly and honestly, without worrying about judgment of any sort at this point. Truthful answers will help you to determine what material you can REALLY discuss in an inspired or passionate manner.

Part 1: Your Activities

If you could only continue ONE of your current activities in college, you would choose: _____

Why?: _____

If you could take up a hobby or activity that you are NOT currently pursuing, you would choose: _____

Why?: _____

Which of your activities has been MOST fulfilling?: _____
_____

Why?: _____

Which of your activities has been LEAST fulfilling?: _____
_____

Why?: _____

In one sentence, what is the most valuable lesson that you have learned from one of your activities?: _____

_____

_____

Part 2: Your Personality

If you had to pick ONLY THREE of your personal strengths, what would they be? Select and circle three (or fewer) terms from the list below and trust your first instincts; DO NOT over-think this writing task.

Resilient	Patient	Outspoken
Creative	Entrepreneurial	Empathetic
Sociable	Self-Aware	Spontaneous
Versatile	Loyal	Pragmatic

Self-Sacrificing   Able to Accept Criticism

Calm under Pressure   Capable of Transformation

Eager to Take Risks   Fascinated by New Ideas

The Profile-at-a-Glance
QUESTIONNAIRE

DIRECTIONS: Respond to the questions quickly and honestly, without worrying about judgment of any sort at this point. Truthful answers will help you to determine what material you can REALLY discuss in an inspired or passionate manner.

Part 1: Your Activities

If you could only continue ONE of your current activities in college, you would choose: _____

Why?: _____

If you could take up a hobby or activity that you are NOT currently pursuing, you would choose: _____

Why?: _____

Which of your activities has been MOST fulfilling?: _____
_____

Why?: _____

Which of your activities has been LEAST fulfilling?: _____
_____

Why?: _____

In one sentence, what is the most valuable lesson that you have learned from one of your activities?: _____

_____

_____

Part 2: Your Personality

If you had to pick ONLY THREE of your personal strengths, what would they be? Select and circle three (or fewer) terms from the list below and trust your first instincts; DO NOT over-think this writing task.

Resilient	Patient	Outspoken
Creative	Entrepreneurial	Empathetic
Sociable	Self-Aware	Spontaneous
Versatile	Loyal	Pragmatic

Self-Sacrificing   Able to Accept Criticism

Calm under Pressure   Capable of Transformation

Eager to Take Risks   Fascinated by New Ideas

The Proofreading Checklist

Does your essay successfully meet the following criteria in terms of writing style?

_____ Relatively advanced but not showy vocabulary

_____ Variety of sentence structures and openings

_____ Differences in sentence length and punctuation

_____ Proper transitions from idea to idea

_____ NO spelling or punctuation errors that would be easily caught with a program like Grammarly

---

If you have time, check through the essay to see if you have avoided the following more obscure grammar problems. Some are covered in this book; others are addressed at length in the PrepVantage SAT series.

_____ No misplaced modifiers or unclear pronouns

_____ No pronoun or possessive pronoun problems ("it" vs "they", "its" vs "it's", etc.)

_____ Proper uses of semicolons, colons, and dashes

_____ Proper uses of words for countable items (number, many, fewer) and non-countable quantities (amount, much, less)

The Second Opinion Checklist

Find a reader who will give you honest responses to the following questions, then ask him or her to complete this questionnaire.

- How many vivid and impressive descriptions or details did you find in this essay? UNDERLINE them in the draft, add up, and choose from below.

0-3 (awful)   4-8 (decent)   9 or more (awesome)

* * *

How many times did you do the following while reading the essay?

laugh: ____   cheer: ____   feel enlightened: ____

If the total number of times for these three actions is lower than 5, the essay MUST be revised.

* * *

- In one sentence, what is the message of this essay?

_____

_____

- In one sentence, what sets this applicant apart from other applicants with _____ as a topic and _____ as a main character trait?

_____

_____

If you cannot quickly provide a single clear sentence for either question, the essay MUST be revised.

The Proofreading Checklist

Does your essay successfully meet the following criteria in terms of writing style?

_____ Relatively advanced but not showy vocabulary

_____ Variety of sentence structures and openings

_____ Differences in sentence length and punctuation

_____ Proper transitions from idea to idea

_____ NO spelling or punctuation errors that would be easily caught with a program like Grammarly

---

If you have time, check through the essay to see if you have avoided the following more obscure grammar problems. Some are covered in this book; others are addressed at length in the PrepVantage SAT series.

_____ No misplaced modifiers or unclear pronouns

_____ No pronoun or possessive pronoun problems ("it" vs "they", "its" vs "it's", etc.)

_____ Proper uses of semicolons, colons, and dashes

_____ Proper uses of words for countable items (number, many, fewer) and non-countable quantities (amount, much, less)

The Second Opinion Checklist

Find a reader who will give you honest responses to the following questions, then ask him or her to complete this questionnaire.

- How many vivid and impressive descriptions or details did you find in this essay? UNDERLINE them in the draft, add up, and choose from below.

0-3 (awful)   4-8 (decent)   9 or more (awesome)

* * *

How many times did you do the following while reading the essay?

laugh: ____   cheer: ____   feel enlightened: ____

If the total number of times for these three actions is lower than 5, the essay MUST be revised.

* * *

- In one sentence, what is the message of this essay?

_____

_____

- In one sentence, what sets this applicant apart from other applicants with _____ as a topic and _____ as a main character trait?

_____

_____

If you cannot quickly provide a single clear sentence for either question, the essay MUST be revised.

The Quirk Questionnaire

- According to your FRIENDS, what is the weirdest thing about you?

  _____

- According to your FAMILY, what is the weirdest thing about you?

  _____

- What hobbies, interests, collections, or obsessions do you have that you mentioned NOWHERE in Chapter 1?

  _____

  _____

  ....

- If you could spend a day doing ANYTHING, what would you do?

  _____

  _____

- What is the strangest thing you have ever done?

  _____

  _____

Name your favorite . . .

Food: _____   TV Show/Film: _____

Band: _____   Way to Relax: _____

The Quirk Questionnaire

- According to your FRIENDS, what is the weirdest thing about you?

  _____

- According to your FAMILY, what is the weirdest thing about you?

  _____

- What hobbies, interests, collections, or obsessions do you have that you mentioned NOWHERE in Chapter 1?

  _____

  _____

  ....

- If you could spend a day doing ANYTHING, what would you do?

  _____

  _____

- What is the strangest thing you have ever done?

  _____

  _____

Name your favorite . . .

Food: _____   TV Show/Film: _____

Band: _____   Way to Relax: _____

The Supplemental Essay Questionnaire

- List three IMPORTANT and LESSER-KNOWN facts about the college that you are discussing.

  1. _____

  2. _____

  3. _____

- Why do you want to go to this college (one phrase or sentence)?

  _____

  _____

- Why is your personality a good fit for your desired college (one phrase or sentence)?

  _____

  _____

- List three INTERESTING EVENTS from your life. Each one must be related to your major.

  1. _____

  2. _____

  3. _____

- Why are you gravitating to this major, and why is it a good fit for your personality (one phrase or sentence)?

  _____

  _____

The Supplemental Essay Questionnaire

- List three IMPORTANT and LESSER-KNOWN facts about the college that you are discussing.

1. _____

2. _____

3. _____

- Why do you want to go to this college (one phrase or sentence)?

_____

_____

- Why is your personality a good fit for your desired college (one phrase or sentence)?

_____

_____

- List three INTERESTING EVENTS from your life. Each one must be related to your major.

1. _____

2. _____

3. _____

- Why are you gravitating to this major, and why is it a good fit for your personality (one phrase or sentence)?

_____

_____

The Supplemental Essay Questionnaire

- List three IMPORTANT and LESSER-KNOWN facts about the college that you are discussing.

  1. _____

  2. _____

  3. _____

- Why do you want to go to this college (one phrase or sentence)?

  _____

  _____

- Why is your personality a good fit for your desired college (one phrase or sentence)?

  _____

  _____

- List three INTERESTING EVENTS from your life. Each one must be related to your major.

  1. _____

  2. _____

  3. _____

- Why are you gravitating to this major, and why is it a good fit for your personality (one phrase or sentence)?

  _____

  _____

The Supplemental Essay Questionnaire

- List three IMPORTANT and LESSER-KNOWN facts about the college that you are discussing.

1. _____

2. _____

3. _____

- Why do you want to go to this college (one phrase or sentence)?

_____

_____

- Why is your personality a good fit for your desired college (one phrase or sentence)?

_____

_____

- List three INTERESTING EVENTS from your life. Each one must be related to your major.

1. _____

2. _____

3. _____

- Why are you gravitating to this major, and why is it a good fit for your personality (one phrase or sentence)?

_____

_____

131

Made in the USA
Middletown, DE
22 October 2020

22603220R00077